I0419988

QUEST
FOR
DIGNITY

SYNTHESIZING IN INDIAN REVIVAL

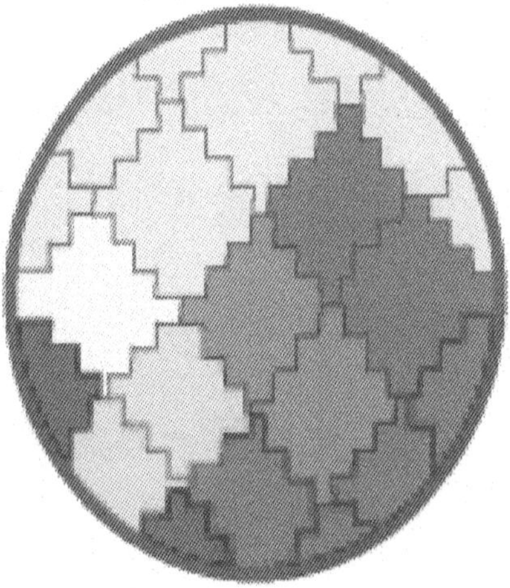

QUEST
FOR
DIGNITY

SYNTHESIZING IN INDIAN REVIVAL

GARY JOSEPH

About the Book

This book is about race relations as it pertains to Native Americans and views of their alcoholism, drug addiction, violence, poverty, etc. Cultural oppression is part of American Society and racism has created spiritual illness, which requires spiritual solution.

- Gary Joseph

TABLE OF CONTENTS

Coyote With No Song

Coyote ran proudly with a deer leg bone in his mouth. He stopped abruptly, and dropped the bone, because he lost track of what he was doing. "What the heck was I going to do?" He sat pondering his situation. "How long has this been going on? Was there someone I am to talk to? Am I doing something of grand importance? It seems so! I think maybe I'm a person who is really important. Some days my thoughts are almost clear, they almost make sense . . . I think I've been confused for a long time."

Coyote got this tremendous itch, and he scratched, only to realize his once beautiful coat was mangy. There were faint wisps of memory, of livelier times, when he was more impressively clad. He looked at the leg bone he was dragging around, and it occurred to him, "Hey this is carrion!" - It seems like I was a hunter at one time! If I were a hunter, did I hunt deer?" A dog appeared in the distance, and saw him, and started running directly at him, yelling crazily, "Get out of here, you chicken thief!" An unreasonable terror gripped Coyote and he ran for his life.

After a while he rested. "Why do I run from him? I could easily cripple or kill him." Coyote realized he was having one of those days. His memories kept on the periphery of his consciousness, maddening, and tantalizing his awareness.

Remembrances drifted close, but without substance or clarity. "This is bad as the itch," he moped as he sat again to ponder. "That dog was not from the forest! . . . What is a chicken? . . . What is a thief? . . . It seems like I'm supposed to be doing something. I just can't focus or concentrate . . .. "

He was assaulted by a tremendous melancholy he could no longer stand. He just flopped down in the brush. The pain of it made him pant, as he lay eye-ball to a blade of grass. " Why am I so depressed? What is this terror that grips me? There is something important to me that is missing! Oh if only I could...."

Then he remembered the chickens. There was a place where strangers to the land and forest lived. They kept chickens there, and when Coyote got hungry all he had to do was take one. He no longer had to hunt, for he just took a dumb chicken. The pain eased a bit and he was able to sit up, Coyote made a joke to himself, "I'm no chicken thief, I'm a great chicken hunter!"

In another moment of realization Coyote knew that insights didn't come as often as they used to. Those memories that almost appeared in his mind triggered a powerful sadness in him. Before this period of almost clear thought fades away, Coyote wonders to himself, "Should I hunt that dog, or should I hunt the chicken?" He has a good belly laugh at the haunting irony of it all.

Now however, he felt compelled to sing, and he lifted his nose to the sky. Through the sounds produced, he expressed what was in the Coyote heart and soul.

He had one of the most beautiful songs in the world, but part of it he lost. Everybody had a song to sing, but part of his was missing. Now he sang every time the spirit moved him. He sang with all his heart. He sang to the sage-brush, he sang to the sky and sun, he sang to the trees, and he sang to that thief Raven, who might be listening. He knew if he sang diligently, he wouldn't lose any more of his song, and that part missing might return.

The beauty of what remained was a haunting reminder of what he had lost. It created the painful emptiness in his gut. Like hunger pangs he longed for that part missing. He knew singing would bring the beauty of the missing part back, he knew he would become complete again. But it was in desperation that he sang.

Wy'! "Hello! or Greetings!"

Ste mas Spoos!? "What is in your heart?" When our people met each other once upon a time, this was the way they used to greet each other. One rarely hears people say these things to each other anymore. It is mostly because we are less open and trusting of each other. The latter was also a form of greeting on meeting someone. "What do you think?", or "What is on your mind?", which are similar, are found in the way the average American initiates conversations. These seem to be questions between familiars or intimates.

So what is in your heart? What is there, that you would be curious about what I would have to say? I am hopeful it would to be something that touches my heart these last few years.

I am much concerned about our people. By our people I mean the Native Americans on this continent. I am told that I am an Indian. I have come to believe that I am an Indian, because, my parents and grandparent told me to be proud that I am such. Also because there have been too many non-Indians that have used the color of my skin to justify treating me with a lack of respect. So in defiance I choose to use this fact as a badge of honor. This sort of defiance is as much a part of my makeup as is a painful self-consciousness about being Indian. This same feeling has come about because my color will invariably lead to some negative outcomes, of some sort or the other, for my life.

I value the good American life. The culture of mainstream America is also who I am. There is not a part of the culture that I don't understand or in which I do not particpate, or perhaps even appreciate. But there is not a day that goes by that I do not feel like a visitor or guest in my own home.

I have been informed that people who will find themselves reading this material, will want to know something about the writer. The most succinct statement I can make about myself, is that, I am an Indian in White America. Much of my education, religious and civic development, assimilation into the American culture, has been directed towards helping me forget or ignore the best of what I am.

Describing who I am begins with this process of making me forget. Saint Mary's Mission was the earliest beginnings of my receiving the culture that I now have. This was a Catholic boarding school for Indians, which has existed longer than the State of Washington. There were Dominican Nuns at St. Mary's, who taught me that I was descended from people who were pagans. This same school, that I came to love and remember with great affection, participated in destroying our language, our prayers, our dances, and many of our ceremonies. Paradoxically, these were replaced with some very beautiful language, ceremonies, prayers, dances and songs from Catholicism. And these form much of the foundation of the way I think and feel today, much of the way I express myself, and to a large degree, my perceptions.

Somehow St. Mary's conveyed on me a whole bag of contradictory and conflicting feelings and ideas about my ancestry. The above mentioned self consciousness and confusion was probably born of a sense of shame and guilt that I believe is generational. Over the years at this school were little reminders that "that is not the way we do things, or that is not the way we are!" The guilt probably comes from not buying into the doctrines completely. For my part at least, there was always some reservation about being part of a lost people needing civilizing.

I was born in a BIA hospital on the Colville Indian Reservation, as were my two brothers and three sisters. This same BIA provided part time employment, annually, to my grandfather, who raised me. The BIA also gave me my first real meaningful employment as a youngster, fighting forest and range fires. Much of my high schooling was also provided by the BIA, and at the time I thought I was real fortunate. Later on in life the BIA would contribute to my college education.

My parents were divorced when I was four years old. After that I lived with various aunts and uncles, until finally I was

4

settled in with my grandparents. I would meet many other children at St. Mary's, who share a similar experience. I would also find that many of our reservation residents experienced or lived through the same circumstances.

From the time I was nine years old, until I graduated from high-school, when I was seventeen-almost eighteen, I lived away from home. I was home during the summer and during various other holiday vacations. I grew up in what I was later to come to know as residential school. If you don't know any better it is pretty good.

I was home during the summer, this is when I got to know my grandparents, aunts and uncles real well. During this time I was being taught about my ancestors and their ways of living, that were totally different from the way I lived the rest of the time. These were exciting and adventurous times.

I learned to hunt deer, bear, grouse, and other small game. I learned how to spear salmon. My family passed on knowledge of the seasons when these sources of food were to be found. My grandmother passed on the family lore about the right time for the roots, berries and other wild harvests. She also showed me and the rest of the extended family where to find these delectables.

When I was around the family, I learned the singing that accompanied the Chinook Dances, and the Stick-Game. It seems that learning to sing, happens at the same time one learns to talk. I was also told that songs were for special purposes. There were people who sang these songs, before our time who sang these songs with great power, for affecting our health and good fortune. I was also told that we no longer had this power. Somehow, somewhere, we lost it.

When the songs were being taught, there were also lessons about where these songs originated. And one can begin to fathom the confusion for a youngster. For a while I didn't understand, "if these songs came from way over there! Why don't we sing songs that come from here?" It is puzzling, that my grandparents came from way over there, but my parents came from over here! That was some very wonderful country where my grandparents came from! Why didn't we live there?

I have come to love this land where we are currently. Anyone who is taught that everything comes from the land, will come to love the land. There is power and spirits in this land. Our songs brought us into a relationship with these spirits and power, a relationship with the land. Even when comparing the grandeur of the Cascades Mountains, or the verdant forests around Lake Wenatchee, there was a sense that even here, we lived amongst awesome beauty.

I left home when I was nineteen, and I sorely missed the sage brush, pine trees, the canyons, the coulees, and mountains where I grew up.

The United States Marine Corps was the next episode in the adventure of my life. By some strange coincidence, I couldn't join the Army when I first enlisted. But once I signed with the good ol' USMC, I was gone within three days. They told me it was my priviledge to be the first to fight and possibly die for may country. It is a strong possibility the Marine Corps, has had as profound an effect on my beliefs and values, as did the Catholic Church. So there I was, a young innocent Indian, ignorant and ready to die if necessary, for my beloved country.

There were some times that I was convinced I would die, although from a hangover rather than in combat. And here, like many Indians, I confronted the central theme of my life, alcohol. It took me years to realize that I was taught to be a drunk. And it took me years to overcome the effects of this destructive element of my life. But because of this alcohol, "by the Grace of God," I find myself on this path that is so rewarding and fulfilling. Although it wasn't without having to overcome some almost insurmountable challenges.

This alcohol, was part of my socialization, from the time I was eleven, until I was twenty-eight. I spent much of my time in taverns and bars. I spent much of my time socializing, in a daze. I got married and divorced within a short year. I came close to suicide from being depressed over my failed marriage, over an empty life, with no purpose and direction to help me. The legal system saved my life.

In early 1978 I was ordered by our Tribal Court to go to alcoholic treatement. That was so humiliating, being called an

6

alcoholic. Yet an honest recognition that I had this condition, also led to my freedom. It led me past religion in search for meaning in my life. Because, although the Catholic Church gave me the means to pray and worship in a meaningful way, I found within myself, resentment, over the shame and guilt I had for being Indian.

My life of sobriety and the spiritual growth helped me to eventually come to terms with that very problem. I started to wonder why so many of my family, community, and all Indian people seem to go through the same thing I had gone through. It took me years of having this predicament, that it occured to me that alcoholism is a symptom. It later may have become a contributing cause to many of my problems. But something else was at the root of my problems. This something else caused a mass infection of my people, Indian people.

Being a person who lived in this country all of his life, I am a product of many contradictions and paradoxes. I can feel comfortable around non-Indians, and accepted, until someone lets me know otherwise. I identify so completely with my countryman brothers.

So when I honestly look at myself, I am no different than many of the people I resent. I am bigoted as anybody. I will discriminate and hate based on a generalization, on a stereotype, of an entire people. I am as narrow-minded and close minded as anyone else when it comes to considering that differing values and beliefs are as valid as my own. I can be as self-righteous and sanctimonious, when my deeply held beliefs are threatened. But believe it or not, I have as much patriotism as anyone. I have as much nationalistic pride. I'm also like many Americans, a chauvanist.

I wasn't any longer, some niaive boy ready to die for his country, I had something I valued more than life from this country in which I was born. And yet the priviledge of dying for it, may have been the only priviledge granted to someone like me willingly. I would be excluded from the rest.

So what is in my heart, is what is in most Americans' hearts. This great culture has given me the sense that I can achieve beyond my wildest imaginings. Somehow I have gained the idea that my potential is limited only by myself. Yet sometimes I resent the obstacles put in place by Americans, white Americans.

I have all the wants and needs of most Americans, but there is a good possibility, that I don't have all the opportunities of most Americans. If one were to look closely at my situation, it is better than most of the rest of the world. Yet I have to put up with assaults on my dignity, and insults to my humanity. These come in the forms directed and focused on my pride.

Lately I have found a source of strength and resilience. I have found a fountain of energy to meet the challenges of being a non-white in this American society. For many years like my brothers and sisters, I tried to fit in. I tried to find approval in the eyes of my non-Indian brothers and sisters.

What is in my heart is goodness I didn't know existed. What is in my heart is the validation of my intrinsic worth to myself, from myself. What is in my heart is a means to differentiate myself, as means to pass on values and beliefs to my offspring, that are life-giving. What is in my heart is hope for the prospect that we can end generations of alcoholism, violence, poverty, and broken families. What is in my heart is the desire to share with my brothers and sisters the means find a purpose and direction in this life here and now.

The system doesn't take what I have to say seriously. I was told that I have to be an expert in the things I will attempt to convey. A college degree, and an advanced degree at that, is required to be an expert in the subject about which I writing. I am an expert! I, being the expert subject, as opposed to being an objective observer. I don't think there are experts, that the system approves of, with degrees who understand racism, from the victims viewpoint. I don't think there are experts, with degrees, who understand poverty and violence from first hand exerience as someone who lives in that environment. The social system has standards that refuse to consider someone who does not have a certificate saying one is an expert in the field, or someone educated in the field. The system demands that the problem of Indian people be dealt with in terms of economics, or psychology, or mental health. Our people were the subjects of genocide, who are the experts on this problem? Our people had our culture dismantled, is this taught in our educational system? I am an expert on living in this type of environment. Many of the readers will understand if I say I have a "P.H.D. from the School of Hard Knocks".

Why doesn't the system understand that some experts in important wisdom and knowledge don't come through our educational system? Why don't they understand that there are some important aspects of our lives, that are healthful and healing, whose existance the dominant system will deny? It is a symptom of our society that represents the ethnocentricity of mainstream American society, that only non-Indians are recognized as experts on Indians. These are the only people who have the certification and degress acceptable to the system.

I come on a quest too that demands that we confront and overcome ignorance and narrow mindedness among our own people. It is this attitude that the things of value come only from the white society. Although there is much there that is priceless from this part of our society, there is also much there that is deadly to my people. And having come through this healing process, I don't need to be certified to share it with my people. Although many of my own people are also convinced that nothing of value can come from Indians, unless it has the approval of non-Indians.

Reservation Pathos

There is going to be some disagreement over what constitutes being an Indian. In our discussion we will focus on the "being" portion, and not so much the legal definition. Much of what is written about in the following pages, deals with Indians as society decides who they are. In many cases this is done to the detriment of the individual. Many in their hearts, will easily identify with, that which is disclosed in this writing, and in their hearts they will know who is Indian. How the majority of our Indian people have dealt with or failed to deal with this situation, will be the topic of our discussion.

The significance of Coyote is that He is a metaphor for our people. He was sent by the Maker to be the Changer and the Trickster of legend and myth. For now he is in a state of confusion and has lost his way. Just as we, who come wandering out of our own bewilderment.

The loss of part of a song is significant in that it represents a loss of part of our spirituality. It isn't to say Indians have misplaced their songs, however we can claim that the songs were taken from us. These were part of the prayers, ceremonies, and language we were forbidden to use. And their use was to keep us healthy and strong. So there were some evil intentions behind the sort actions that destroyed our way of praying.

Indians understand that the song is a gift from the spiritual realm. A person is gifted a song after an encounter with the spirit helpers, after making oneself worthy. Also the song may have been passed on along the spirituality represented by that song. We have lost much of our songs, and we have lost much that is associated with those songs. Much of the spirituality that gave vitality to our people is greatly missing.

Now our people are like drunks, awakening from being passed out after a long party, with a serious hang over. We have started to take the measure of our surroundings, where we've

10

been hibernating. As with most drunks, we wake up remorseful, for squandering some more of this precious gift of life. I'm awakening, and with my new found awareness, I'm making shocking discoveries about our people. I have come to understand the full implication that over half of our people live in depressing poverty, defeated and demoralized. Like a revelation, this has come to me. The condition has always existed, but I never really took what it meant to heart. People like me see the problems and presume, somebody else must be doing something to address them. Most have simply resigned to the fact that this is the way things are supposedly meant to be. Some   recognize   the   insurmountable   challenges   being confronted, trying to help or alleviate the pain of our people. Most of these poor and unemployed are the full-blooded Indian members of our tribe.

I'm just another one of those people who have been asleep too long, awakened rudely by disturbing dreams. And I was trying to interpret a dream, and in that dream, most of our people went and moved away from the main camp, and went to camp in the hard place. They were treated badly, their feelings deeply hurt,   and   there   was   a   tremendous   sense   of   oppression, deprivation and separation. Another part of this drama was that we wouldn't be complete people, until we reconciled with those in the hard place. There have been other dreams and visions just as bothersome.

It's possible I'll just be reconciling part of myself that has been buried and ignored. Maybe I need to bring the Indian in me home and honor that person, that part of me that for so long also went away and camped in that hard place.

A part of me is with the people who went to camp in that hard place. Those that have stayed are better off economically and socially, so to speak. But I can't get over the idea that a grievous sin has been committed against those people camped in that hard place. The making of the tribe complete seems to require the redemption of those in the main camp. Once this has occurred, the people in that hard place will return.

But now that the thought is there, it won't go away I fear, unless I act on it.

Like many of the men in my generation and those who lived prior to it, I can count on one hand the times that I've cried in the last fifteen years. There were the funerals of my grandfather and my father. The other times, when I started actively praying, another was when I finished a Cursillo, and finally recently, when I tried a new way of praying. The only other time was when I was jogging and thinking about the dream, and the idea struck forcefully, about the people in that hard place. I could feel emotion build up along with the awareness, as I was at about three and a half miles out, finally it just burst out of me. It still isn't quite clear just what exactly are those people of ours in that hard place, and what is their meaning intellectually.

I have never been one to foster feelings of the sort that have developed since then. All along I must have known how difficult life is around here. But there exists within me a defense mechanism called indifference. Now something has rattled my blinders, and I've gotten a glimpse of reality.

On taking a closer and closer examination of "those people," one discovers that they endure some terrific hardships. I have this premonition that they are being sacrificed. Inactivity and neglect, by those who could or should help, keeps these people in that hard place. The efforts aren't overt, mostly various indifferent people have the conviction that the people there, deserve or want to be there. There seems to be a consensus, that to try and change their situation is futile. Some brave souls have broken their own hearts and spirits trying to change things. There have been churches, social programs, and government programs, all have tried bring about change. All have given up on the people in that hard place. Those people in that hard place, have given up on themselves. The hard place is rock hard apathy.

Alcoholism, drug abuse, family dysfunction, compulsive gambling, chronic unemployment, and a willingness to meet challenges with violence, are the environment of those people in that hard place. In this hard place, there is no dignity. At first I felt pity for them, but pity violates them more than their own apathy, or the indifference of the rest of the tribe. As I become more enlightened about their condition, love and compassion felt

12

for them, overrides the defensive indifference.

I once read a book called "Lame Deer Seeker of Visions." He recounts about seeing t-shirts with silk screen printing on them, "Custer died for your sins." He counters however that Custer didn't die, he goes on living, in the cattle-rancher, in law enforcement, in the government, in the BIA, and even in our own tribal councils and tribal governments. A part of me knows that indeed this is the truth.

Twenty years ago when it seemed fashionable, I read this book. I recall Lame Deer's involvement in various Indian non-violent, Indian civil disobedience, and Indian protest activities. AIM had caught our imagination and Wounded Knee was about to happen again.

Recently I read that book again. I totally misunderstood its main point the first time I read it. Completely overlooked was the man's spirituality. Now however, I can see and comprehend another's spirituality. Maybe, what our people in that hard place are waiting for, is what Lame Deer brings to light.

I just got re-acquainted with a fellow named George Abrahamson. In our first discussion I claimed the problems our people faced were caused by racism over the years. He agreed that the problems may be caused by racism. Strangely enough, he was very careful about putting forth solutions. Racism and its results, he told me, were illness or sickness, to be treated by a spiritual means. The remedy for racism and its effects, was to make people healthy and wholesome.

I have argued that the problems of alcoholism, unemployment, dysfunctional families, compulsive gambling, and violence are symptoms of deeper problems. The cause was our own inability to accept, approve, and love ourselves. Racism, was what brought these conditions into our lives.

Healing and spirituality, -- these are very comforting words. George is probably right about making our people healthy and wholesome.

Lame Deer was right in saying Custer was still alive. The worst offenders against the dignity of our people are our own leadership, and their various managers and administrators. Almost every person who happens to discuss the attitudes of members that control our tribal council, comment that they, these controlling members of the council, don't believe in their fellow Indians. They don't value the hopes and aspirations of the Indians, couldn't care less about their feelings on unemployment, alcoholism, and poverty. These council members will always view our Indians as peons, and as unimportant people. What does this say about the people who elect these people repeatedly? It is a symptom also, of a deep problem.

If anything will inhibit necessary changes for our people, it is the self-centeredness and self-importance of our leadership. They are too concerned with their public image to provide a vision for the long term, for our people. No person in a leadership position in our Tribe, has been educated, but they've surrounded themselves with non-Indians who are. So the solutions to our problems, as viewed by our leadership, have a familiar insensitivity to them about Indians.

Those Indians that are being brought into the circles of leadership have the same smug sense of superiority and sanctimony about them. They have learned how to "interface" with Indians. They know how talk legalese, and the latest bureaucratic buzz words, but they know nothing about speaking and listening from the heart. Our leadership should take a moment for consideration; fifty-seven percent of our people on the reservation are unemployed; forty percent of the people employed by the Tribal government, BIA, and our enterprises, are non-Indian; seventy-five percent of the managers in the Tribal government, Tribal enterprises, and BIA, are non-Indians. Who are we working for?

As I mentioned, managers and administrators around here also carry on in the spirit of Custer. Some of them seem honestly convinced that Indians are non-competants. As a way to differentiate these Indians, these surrogate Custers, they are referred to as apples, red on the outside, white on the inside. I suspect some of them are just rotten to the core. But looking at it honestly, they are behaving the way they were taught, the way they were conditioned by society.

George has a mentor named Melvin, who says that the Indians' main problem is jealousy toward other Indians. And I

14

have to confess, there is a good possibility I'm jealous and envious. My personal sense of self-righteousness tells me that I should have more status and prestige, more money, more property, more "things". I'm learning though, and I'm probably better off without these things. It would be erroneous, however, to let that jealousy and envy, cancel out any honest and legitimate anger over indignity and injustice. Jealousy is a symptom along the path of a series of symptoms, of a much deeper problem.

It does seem like strange good fortune to come across these two gentleman when I'm searching for the type of answers they can provide. It certainly is heartening to me, to come across people involved in their type of work to be sincere, honest, and humble. There are people around here trying Indian spirituality, who lack this distinctive sincerity and humility.

George has talked about Indians from all over the United States and Canada congregating at a place called Bear Butte. It is supposed to be a sacred place to the Plains Indians. He said he had been going there for seven years now, and the gatherings get bigger and bigger each year. They come there so they can do a vision quest. We've had that as part of our cultural heritage, probably hasn't been in much use lately though. The possibility that more and more people are doing a vision quest is intriguing. What would cause them to try that particular activity? My first thought, when told of this vision quest was, "A whole night by myself on top of mountain, -in the dark! ..." That's what happens, and it builds up to fours nights on the mountain. George tells me that in Melvin's language, the word for the vision quest translates into, "To meet one's true self, or get to know the true self." This has profound implications for helping our people.

I suspect he is right in that the route to the solution to the root of our problems is making our people healthy and wholesome. Hopefully I'm not grasping at straws, but I suspect we'll be examining this vision quest thing, up close and personal. From a ridge, say maybe in the South Nanamkin, we'll look over and see friendly co-travelers of the spiritual path, on Bear Butte.

The attractive feature of George's revelation is the Indians are searching the ceremonies and rituals of their cultural religions.   Melvin and Lame Deer both emphasize that differences among tribes should be ignored, similarities and strengths emphasized, and re-establishing Indian spiritual practices among the Indians on the reservations. So we embark on a quest to remember and rediscover those activities that kept our people healthy. And we keep our ears to the ground, and listen with our hearts, for messages that will have to come through time from previous generations. So effective has been the effort to eradicate our culture, all we have are fragments of the map our ancestors used.

Preliminary Analysis

The first thing I wanted to do was to develop a cursory analysis, take the most obvious situations without a detailed examination, and report on them. I have to admit that given the subjectivity of the claims made, that it is more rabble-rousing and propaganda, than objective analysis. It is an expression of self-righteous indignation, over a creeping awareness of what it is that is killing our people off.

My first serious and honest examination of the conditions faced by our people begins. It started when I saw an application to a wonderful grant called "Healthy Nations." I was encouraged that we had good chance of getting the grant. A social worker told me however, to qualify the reservation had to be a pretty bad place for young people to grow up. There was a high probability we would submit a successful application for this particular grant.

I feel compelled to express these conclusions and views because I am convinced that our leadership and government lack a vision for all of our Indian people. They have no strategy for bringing our people out of the devastation brought about by the destruction of our culture. There is no vision because our people lack vision. One reason is those that keep and maintain the principles of our forebears, are viewed by those in power, as "Non-competants," to use the BIA euphemism. Somehow they managed to convey this idea to us. Which we accepted!

To quote policies put forth by our Tribal government, "The continuing strategy for all Tribal activities is to be self-determinant and economically self-sufficient." What is missing here is an understanding of what constitutes the nature of the "self." This missing element about our concept of ourselves will constantly resurface as the fundamental characteristic of the problem confronting our people. It will also figure into the proposed solution to those problems.

So, let us assess and measure how successful the Tribe is in its quest to be self-determinant and self-sufficient. Again a caution, the measurements are from the heart.

Self determination would have to mean in this case, that the Tribe will be the sole arbiter and maintains responsibility for factors under its sovereign domain. A conclusion we can safely draw is that a nation that will be self-determinant and self-sufficient, will have to have people that are individually self-determinant and self-sufficient.

Let's borrow a procedure from the business strategists and marketing people, called a SWOT analysis. This is a process where the strengths, weaknesses, opportunities, and threats to the Tribes' overall goals and objectives, are analyzed. For purposes of identifying priorities we'll glance at weaknesses and threats. To do this is a matter of looking at areas of obvious concern to the Tribe, stated in a series of soul searching and introspective questions.

Areas of concern, would address improving the quality of life for members of our community. In political self determination, an area of concern is the membership participation in the political process, by voting or running for elected office. In the development of human capital, concern would be over the completion of education, its availability, its utility, and are we getting fullest potential benefit. Social ill concerns could be the incidences of compulsive behavior disorders, alcohol, gambling, or drugs. Is the basic social unit, the family, healthy? Is there a high incidence of domestic violence, a high divorce rate, or the incidence of single parent households? Are our institutions producing tomorrow's leaders?

Can the Tribe claim to be self-determinant if less than 75% of tribal members vote for their leadership? Can a vocal and active minority truly represent the whole? Can we be sure half of our people aren't conditioned to helplessness? If a people are conditioned to helplessness, is it morally or ethically correct for those that work and vote, to act without finding out the concerns of the majority?

If we were to ask these questions about an individual, could we not safely conclude that the individual is not functioning to the full extent of individual capacity? As a sovereignty, are we functioning at the full extent of our capabilities?

When we look at the case for self-sufficiency, we end up rating ourselves even lower. Can we claim self-sufficiency with the huge roster of people on public assistance or unemployment compensation? If over half of our people are living in poverty, what does this say about the focus of our efforts and expenses? We developed enterprises to address unemployment. The same people unemployed back when the enterprises were initiated, are still the same ones unemployed now! It looks like we totally misunderstood the seriousness of the breadth and depth, or the very nature of our problem. Unemployment is so pervasive on the reservation it seems various institutions find it an acceptable condition of life.

If it were in our power to make everyone vote, -make everyone take a job, -force everyone to quit drinking, drugging or gambling, we would only be removing symptoms, and not solving the fundamental problem. If an individual displays symptoms of an illness such as fever, we'd be negligent if we only gave that person aspirin to reduce fever. Suppose there is an infection that causes the fever? Can we in all honesty say that our solutions to problems all deal with the real causes of problems and not just the symptoms? Treat the causes and the symptoms abate.

Most organizations are at their most basic and fundamental purposes involved in either exploiting opportunities to achieve fulfillment of their purpose, or resolving problems or obstacles that hinder that achievement. With over half of our people camped in a very hard place can we say we're fulfilling our purpose? Is it acceptable to have over 50% unemployment, or to have 70% of our people living below the poverty line?

What is worse, the indifference of those that have it made economically, or the apathy of those mired in the sand trap that is poverty?

One thing to be said of indifference and apathy is that these are symptoms of sickness of the heart. These are symptoms of something very fundamentally wrong. So far it seems that the treatment has been to pretend that these symptoms aren't there.

Various forms of escapism are employed by all to bring about a collective delusion that those people in that hard place, desire, or at the very least, deserve, to be there.

It took a hundred and seventy-five years to get where we're at now. The severest damage to the Tribe has been done in the last hundred or so years. We've been bombarded with an avalanche of misinformation about who we are. The sheer volume of this information has shaped us surely as has water shaped the Grand Coulee and the Big Bend country.

The enculturation of myths in the dominant culture has been imposed on us to justify or to minimize genocide or destruction of entire cultures by the Believers of Manifest Destiny. It is an indoctrination occurring over the years, reflecting what mainstream society wanted to hear on the history of Indians. Over the years we have sat mesmerized by the movies, television, literature, education, religious and social customs, that reinforced the myth of the American Indian. We bought it, and now that is what we call ourselves.

In the clash of cultures, the victor is able to write the history, and has complete freedom of revision to make it more palatable to posterity. The paradigm has been the Indian as being predestined to suffer humiliating defeat to white superiority. This portrayal of superiority, is not only one of superior technology, superior military and political strategy, but of moral superiority. Never mind that the native peoples were defending their homelands, families and way of life, they were an obstacle to the American Way. The history of the removal of this obstacle has been mythologized as a transmission of culture. Out of necessity, it has been rendered as a noble endeavor. So the history portrays exploits of the newcomers as pioneers, instead of trespassers.

The last few decades of the history of the Indian People has mainly been a struggle to find dignity and self respect in a society whose cultural myths demand much less. Who wants to revise the vision of pioneering efforts to one of greed and deception?

Our unemployment, alcoholism, family violence, lack of education, lack of vision, are symptoms of an ailing society.

These symptoms are found in the prevailing American culture but not to the degree of severity found in our local Indian Culture. Has it ever been questioned as to why this is the case? Is our social and economic structure only meant to employ 43% of our employable people? Are the levels of alcoholism and drug abuse meant to be an inherent part of our culture? Is the learned dependance of over 50% of our people our true heritage? Can we claim self determination when too many of us have no choice when we will or will not drink alcohol or take drugs; over the amount knowledge we'll gain this year; how much money we bring home to our families; whether or not our families can stay together? Can we feel empowered when over half our people are apathetic about voting for their elected officials? Can we blame them for being cynical? There is a sense that whomever is elected, there will be no change for those under duress from poverty or ignorance.

The foregoing comments indicate that we have achieved our vision of self determination to a very minimal degree. A solid minority have done very well economically. It is healthy people who give meaning to the management of Tribal assets. But if Indians don't benefit from our assets, who are we managing them for? Are we managing them for a minority population within the Tribe?

An approach to consider for the long term is to develop healthy individuals within the confines of the Reservation through governmental, educational, and religious institutions; recover and rehabilitate those that have fallen victim to social ills such as alcoholism, drug abuse etc.; recover and rehabilitate habitual criminal offenders; educate and train the chronically unemployed. Develop processes that nurture and reinforce cohesive and healthy families; instill and reinforce values conducive to healthy relationships for young people; instill and reinforce values conducive to healthy parenting for young parents; teach methodologies and practices involved in spirituality, meditation, and holistic healing; demand the adherence to high professional, moral, and ethical standards in our institutions, the measure being the integrity of our leadership.

All the above imply going into areas where most institutions fear to tread. Decisions regarding issues of morality have always been in the domain of the individual. But to overcome images of inferiority and inadequacy, or the spirit of helplessness and defeat, may well call for institutionalized efforts in these areas. There will be alarms going off in everyone's heads, concerning infringement on individual choice, but a large part of our membership here and in cities have lost many of those choices already. Being able to make rational choices regarding spiritual, economic, or political well being, are the benchmark of a self determinant people or society.

The challenges we all face in our individual struggles for dignity and self respect center around our perception of who we are. Like many people who contemplate our condition, intuition tells me that we have lost our way, we don't know how to be who we are. The key question to answer is, "Who are we?".

There was a concatenation of a long line of customary behavior patterns that reinforced our identity as a people. Our basic spiritual beliefs were lost during these drastic changes. The way we taught our young people to be responsible contributing members of society disappeared. Our political and economical system of sharing power and wealth whereby the whole family, band, or tribe benefited, was replaced by one of competition for individual power and wealth. The system of competition rewarded and reinforced those behaviors that made the individual more important than the group. Those that couldn't or wouldn't compete, found no alternatives to abdicating their will to act.

The way that the spiritual beliefs were transmitted, the way to function in society, were learned in the family. Look at the generations of alcoholism, look at the generations of unemployability, look at the generations who chose to face challenges violently, and you'll see generations of people coming from broken families. It is rare that we see individuals who come from generations of stable family units. It is our duty to honor the people who survived this tragic process

One of the symptoms of alcoholism and one of the causes for its difficulty in treating it, is the phenomenon of denial.. This denial in not only individual, but community wide, and even institutionalized.

The same claim can be made about healthy families here on the Colville Indian Reservation. When the subject is broached as an innovative approach to dealing with social health problems, unhealthy dysfunctional families and their prevalence is denied. When we want to produce healthy individuals we need to look at the families where these individuals originate. Are these families passing unhealthy behavior patterns generationally?

There is a possibility that a new consensus is emerging stating that most of these problems can be traced to traumatic events in a persons infancy, childhood, and adolescence. The events occurred because parents were passing on dysfunctional behavior. The resultant behaviors passed on to the following generation.

The environment for making dysfunctional individuals was created and maintained in the last 150 years, at least with regard to Indian Peoples. The disruption of families was a practice of the Army and later the BIA as a matter of policy to eradicate Indian Culture. There is a period in time that can be identified when the transmission of cultural values was interrupted to a very serious degree. It is easy to see how this occurred, separate the child from the wisdom of the Elders, tell a child: " You can't speak your language!" "You can't perform your ceremonies the way you normally been used to!" "You can't sing your songs!" - "You can't even tell your stories!" Replace this with new religion, new political processes, new ways to socialize and you end up with different paths to status and prestige, power, and wealth. You have a refraction of goals, to use light as a frame of reference. The basic drives of people are slightly bent, but enough to be disastrous for an entire people.

Would it be presumptuous to say that we are a lost people? A look at the various statistical analyses done up to date would support such a claim. We have an externally imposed concept of who we are culturally and racially, and it is one of inferiority. Generations of well meaning people have come to this reservation to help these "poor misfortunates". It is almost heretical to imply we shouldn't depend on the U. S. Government.

The social fabric of Tribal society is one of dis-unity, factionalism, or fractionated elements. If one could characterize the relationship among its people it would be one of jealousy and suspicion to the point of paranoia. The basic attitude seems to be "I'll have to get my fair share, because there isn't enough to for everyone".

The problem to be solved suggests a very long term approach, perhaps across a number of generations. Each step of the way should emphasize a way to make each person a wholesome and complete human being. Each step should include a holistic approach including physical, mental, emotional, and spiritual health. We should not claim any progress until all persons have made some progress towards completeness. We should recognize that we are a unity, that can only succeed as a unity, because as a unity we are seriously troubled.

Along the lines of the Healthy Nations concept, is the determination made about "what is a healthy nation?" For that matter, will there be a determination of what is a healthy institution or a healthy leadership? The composite of a healthy nation are the healthy individuals within the families, communities, and institutions. Again our attention is drawn to the family, and what constitutes a healthy unit.

To repeat an earlier statement, -any development of strategy will address fundamental questions of purpose, and to answer these questions will direct us to key and critical long term decisions. The decisions made will be our strategy.   A key concern is will the current leadership commit itself to an emphasis or focus in strategy. Once a healthy leadership is determined, what next? The implication all along during this discourse, has been a leadership that lacked a certain consistency in direction. Also the institutions charged with executing the leadership policies are seriously bureaucratized, or dysfunctional. A dysfunctional institution according to various esteemed authorities is one where the institution serves itself rather than the community for which it exists to serve. A symptom of a dysfunctional institution is one where those charged with carrying out the institutional mission, direct its most serious efforts to protecting their individual positions of power and prestige. We have to take a candid look at the values of the voters that keep these people in their positions.

If we step back to the SWOT Analysis and review our strengths and opportunities we then can start to see that there is hope for our people. For all our differences we still share a common experience that forms a tremendously strong bond among us all. We share the poverty, the racial discrimination, the political misfortunes, and the rest of the history that goes with being Indian. It seems, that as a people, we are entering a new phase in the grieving process over our loss of ourselves as a people. There is a surge of strength and vitality that comes with recognition of surviving a catastrophe. Many individuals on the reservation are seeking renewal.

There is a grassroots movement locally to looking at meeting our challenges through spiritual means. People are reviewing the traditional methods of praying and meditating; looking at traditional methods of acquiring and nurturing values for wholesome and healthy living; practicing the dances, games, and social events unique to our culture. And because there was this loss of patterns of living, new customs from the assimilated dominant culture are being integrated with the old that remain. This integration of parts of the old and new are creating new traditions and new culture. As a people we are coming back to living in the present moment.

The opportunity presents itself for us to forge a new identity. Not one based on racial identity, for that one is collectively seen as inferior. A new identity will have to be based on something even more fundamental or more elemental. We've tried Indian, we've tried American, we've tried Native American, we need to try Human Being. All that is ideal in being human needs to be our goal. All that is noble, all the unlimited potential associated with being human is ours already. At the very essence of being human is our spirituality and all that this implies.

What we seem to be doing is seeking a commitment to an intention as opposed to making a decision on the process. We desire to have wishes and aspirations articulated to some degree. These wishes and aspirations can be ideals compared to an honest and candid evaluation of where we are at in the present, from which a vision for posterity must emerge. Through a declaration or manifesto, by consensus, we will articulate who we are as a people. Generally such are the results of a convocation of prayer, meditation, healing, and celebration.

A gathering of tribes has generally preceded the development of nations. The Constitutional Congress of the United States is an example. The Constitution of the USA, is an articulation of who the people of this country aspire to be. It is the manifesto to live by. It is also evolving to fit contemporary situations within the larger world order. It was a rebirth after two hundred years of domination by a foreign power. We should also experience such a rebirth.

I invite those that share a common interest for the identification of the problems we have faced as a people, and brainstorming possible solutions.

An analysis will generally include the resources necessary to provide a solution. There is a small cadre of people who have acquired order and balance in their lives. If we can identify, assemble, and organize the processes these people have used, it is a start at providing a solution. What is common to these people is a total commitment to a spiritual emphasis in their lives.

Shortened Histories

I want to interrupt our train of thought to take a moment of respectful silence in memory the following people who are relatives, acquaintances, and friends. I submit them because others undoubtably could also submit similar if not identical testimonies. Each family on the reservation could present similar if not worse cases.

I will start with my father who died in 1991. He suffered a stroke in 1983, I think from trying to sober up. He was diagnosed with having diabetes, gout, ulcers, high blood pressure, and he was an alcoholic. He divorced my mother when I was four. He had six children with my mother, who are still alive, two daughters preceded him in death, also tragically. He also had two sons outside of his marriage. All his life he was a construction worker, and very proud of his profession. He was a World War II veteran, being in the Army Air Corps as a tail gunner in a B-17 bomber. He participated in eighteen missions over Hitler's Europe before he was shot down. He served about a year and a half as a prisoner of war. In his later years he was a devout Catholic. A rather dignified little man, he had one gripe he confided in me. Until 1955 no non-Indian tavern or store owner would serve him liquor, he felt he earned the right. He knew he had endured too much for this country for it to treat him that way. He died of complications from the stroke.

Lance Whalawitsa was a younger cousin. Grew up on the Warm Springs Indian Reservation. His mother died when he was about two. He was a well paid electrician, or should have been. He thought people pushed him around unnecessarily, bullied and intimidated him, so he came home to the Colville Indian Reservation, where the rest of his huge extended family lived. He once confided in me that he needed help or he would die. He went through a couple of alcohol treatments. He became despondent and depressed, and finally committed

27

suicide.

An aunt Charlotte, died in 1971, of a combination medication and alcohol overdose. She was an alcoholic already subject to DT's.

Rudy McCraigie, boyhood friend, school mate, and later a more distant acquaintance. Drifted into alcoholism. He died at home, of Cirrhosis.

Lawrence McCraigie, brother of Rudy, similar case as Rudy, he died at home of Cirrhosis.

Leona Dick, Wiley, Joseph, stepmother, aunt, spent the last thirty days of her life in intensive care. In her younger days she spent time in a "reformatory for way-ward women" (her words). She had been to three or four alcohol treatment centers for alcoholism. She even quit drinking for a number of years. Her doctor gave up on her. She died from Cirrhosis.

Gene Matt, uncle, was the half brother of my father. Died alone in a motel, two thousand miles away in New Orleans. Called me at work some time shortly before he died, saying he just needed to talk to an Indian.

Francis Condon, cousin, died from stab wounds he sustained in a drunken brawl.

George Condon, cousin, committed suicide.

Sandy Circle, boyhood acquaintance, drinking buddy. Died of Cirrhosis. He had lost his voice, doctors told him to quit drinking or he would die. He chose to keep drinking.

Alan Van Brunt, was a boyhood companion and friend. Later on an acquaintance. Died from injuries sustained from being hit by an auto, sitting in the middle of a highway, probably drunk.

Reggie James, was a boyhood friend, later a drinking buddy. Died in prison trying to drink wood alcohol.

Harry Williams, was a boyhood friend, later an acquaintance. Died in his own wood shed, he committed suicide.

Norman Senator, an acquaintance, probably two years younger than myself, committed suicide.

Winfred Simpson, an acquaintance, probably one year younger than myself, committed suicide.

Louie Simpson, an uncle, committed suicide, by taking off all of his clothing an wandering off into the night, during a snow storm.

Larry Simpson, his younger brother also committed suicide.

Rose Clark, mother-in-law, died in a car wreck, while drinking.

Ronnie Cleoparty, boyhood friend, later on still a part of a circle of friends, died in a car wreck while partying.

Norma Waters, a childhood friend, died in a car wreck, alone, probably drunk.

These are all violent, senseless, useless deaths, involving alcohol. The reason I pause to wonder, is this happened over a period of fifteen or twenty years. It was at time when I was coming out of a fog. Why didn't they find their way out? What strange affliction prevents me from feeling sad for them until 1994? Why is it that some them, who have had the opportunities I was given, didn't take them? I believe they didn't understand the nature of the giving.

Once again we are confronted with the phenomenon of having this inability to feel, as evidenced in the inability to grieve normally. Is it normal to take this long to develop human emotion and feeling that has atrophied? When the causes for death and dying stare us in the face, why don't we act to do something about it? This inability to act and feel are symptoms of apathy. But why does apathy color and flavor the general ambiance of our people?

The general condition of alcoholics on our reservation is a good example. Those being sent to treatment come out with the same question. "Why bother?" Has whatever our people been through completely destroyed their hope for something better? Do they even look for something better?

What Draws Us Together?

Much of what concerns us is the result of an awakening experienced by a number of people on our reservation. It wasn't something that occurred in a flash, but more or less a gradual unfolding. They came together for a rather singular meeting, the assistant chief of police, the social worker, a housing administrator, a BIA realtor, a queen of Indian pageantry, a computer programmer, a forester, and a safety man: John Dick, Albert Andrews, Charlie Gua, Gloria Simpson, John St. Pierre, Lovina Louie, Jeannie Louie, and Gary Joseph. All of them searching for answers to the various questions in life. All of them searching for solutions to challenges that were literally killing off our people. It is by no coincidence that each is convinced the answers and solutions will be found in the example of their own lives. They are determined to examine the possibilities and feed what hope they have. What hope they have is the result of finding the answers and solutions, and applying them to their own conditions individually.

There was the recognition that the solutions and answers found individually were difficult to pass on. Most of the people we knew, refused, to even by the slightest inclination, to apply what we had learned in life, to their own situation. ..."Hey, how am I going to help you, if you keep fighting me off?"

Indian problems, solutions, and strategy, brought to their attention in an essay, mention of dysfunctional families, alcoholism, drug abuse, violence, chronic unemployment, learned helplessness and hopelessness, and an indoctrination of inferiority. It gives a tragic rendoring of the condition of our people, a portrait or snapshot of the social condition on the reservation. Other Indians could identify and empathize with this litany of tragedy and fatality, conditions prevalent on any Indian reservation.

The policeman and the social worker thought the essay was

good, and had said "Lets get more people interested, lets get them to talk about the issues you bring up". The hundredth such group formed to solve the current life crisis, this time, not an exercise in futility, and without the cynicism or despair of the other ninety-nine.   The safety man was always convinced the heart of the problem was racism. Not so much blatant bigotry. Just a habitual display of superiority, patronization, and condescension by the local White People. A respondent display of habitual and learned inadequacy and inferiority by the local Indians. Is it conceivable that our condition is caused by such a seemingly banal condition?

Most of the other attendants thought alcoholism and drug abuse were the main threats to our people. It sure seemed obvious such was the case, anyway. So many deaths in car wrecks and suicides when people got drunk too much. Families disintegrating because the parents got drunk too much. People unable to get and hold a decent job because they got drunk too much. It is entirely possible that people got drunk too much because they hurt too much. That they got drunk too much is a symptom of a need to kill all feeling.

The social worker had a rather interesting perspective. He thought that maybe we were stuck somewhere in the process of grieving.   In the first meeting was mention of us losing something vital to ourselves, but we don't know what we lost. Maybe we grieve over the loss of ourselves. The pschycologists identify various states of grieving that mark the progression of healing from a serious or debilitating pain.   And just maybe somewhere along this progression we were stuck.

In regards to the stages of grieving, of all of the worst possibilities, getting stuck in denial, was the worst. We will never get started into the recovery or healing process. We will go on suffering, meanwhile we will be working on the wrong solution, because we would have identified the wrong cause.

As I said at the root of our problem is racism. The worst aspect associated with this racism, is that many of our people have turned it against other tribal members, -we've turned against our very selves. It appears this is the first stumbling block to healing and recovery. When you're being inflicted the worst hurt possible, you respond with the worst you can muster. It seems the worst hurt imaginable is the denigration of a person's sense of rightness and well being as a human being. "I'm going to make feel less than you really are, ...I'm going to make you feel less than human", they seem to want to say. "The inner sense of your own godliness, that is yours by heritage, is going to be wiped out!"

I honestly believe that racism, grieving, and denial have a relationship in the nature of our problem of apathy. If we honestly examine in ourselves, in our thinking and behavior, the effects from racism, we'll start the progress towards healing. If we grieve the loss of ourselves, our identify, and our dignity, we get on with living. Otherwise I fear we'll be examining and searching until there is no longer any Indians.

Each attendant responded with a soulful and heartfelt, sympathetic and empathetic, testimony of pain. From a profound and eloquent understanding of the experiences catalogued in the essay, came the need to identify with "all these bad things". Mandatory memories, -no one allowed to bury them, -lest we forget and the cycle repeats. It seems someone in our generation forgot, and we worked earnestly and diligently to deaden our own pain.

The things that make us human are the way we socialize, our customs, our relationship to beauty, our expressions of beauty, our relationship to God, our ways we express our relationship to God, and the way we pass on our collective learning. Most in attendance at that meeting sensed the loss of all of these by the majority of people on the reservation.

Each of the respondents was at one time or the other a drunk. With the exception of the policeman and the forester, each had been a widowed or divorced. Of course the pageant queen was too young to have been in such a relationship, yet. The forester claimed his marriage survived by a some fluke he didn't understand. He acknowledged that his wife's insistence that they stay married might have something to do with it.

Many a friend of the people in attendance had died of Cirrhosis or suicide, or a car wreck, or some other pointless incident while drunk. More than one close or intimate loved one had been torn from us each individually and lost forever. In our contemporaries, the roll call of the dead, was getting too large, relative to the roll call of the living.

In the midst of such tragedy, people still found meaning and purpose to their lives. Ours seems to be that we were to become evangelists.

Most of the people present experienced drastic changes in their lives, of a spiritual nature. The turn to spirituality was usually the result of some devastating event in their personal lives. All of them were reborn, or transformed in the spirit. However, rejection of the spiritual journey, from those we were trying to share with, was a rather common experience. Each had tried converting our fellows, twelve stepping them, -or any means to get them to take a look at themselves.

"I see some terrible things I just can't believe! We need to teach these people how to be good human beings! They beat each other up viciously, and don't remember doing it, or why they did it. They have no feeling for each other. ...They've lost something important, they've lost their customary way of treating and relating to family and community. They lost their spirituality, their traditional way of praying and healing. We got to show them a way back to that!" This was from the policeman, obviously the person who would bear witness to most the challenging conditions we would confront. In a moment of fantastic insight, he concluded, "Lets teach these people to be good human beings!" It would certainly change the in-humane things they do to each other.

Each of us suspected that the inherent respect and reverence the targets of our concern had for Indian culture was the key. Intuition told us that getting to the source or cause of the problem would lead us to the solution. The inability to see ourself as worthy of being individually loved by God, other people, or even oneself, was the first obstacle. That we were of value to God, to ourselves, and to others had to come from within ourselves, and not randomly skimmed from the air. This is complicated by the fact that we would have to overcome the very instincts that help people survive the difficulties and challenges we would address.

So how do you convince your own people who were dedicated to a deadly life-style, that it is morbid? How do you convince people dedicated to hedonistic practices that their way is pointless and fraught with emptiness? The way is evident. Enlighten the people, that there is something wrong with their chosen existence. Convince them, that transformation is the most fulfilling and rewarding occurances in anyone's life. Convince them the transformation or renewal comes about as the result of a spiritual quest. That we can identify our goal is simple, how to achieve it is another matter.

Each of those present is convinced that their lives are a miracle. Some think they should have been dead, or in jail, or in the nut house. That their lives are miraculous, they believe, they can translate this miraculous change, into the lives of others among the people. This isn't a fantasy but a real sense of faith and belief that they can accomplish such a feat. Some have mentioned, "Maybe this is our purpose in life."

We touched on the topic that maybe we can show people how to recover their dignity and self-respect. Somehow we're going to convince the people that the way they are carrying on is beneath their dignity as human beings. It does not seem rational or logical to attempt this, but there is nothing rational or logical about miracles. Spiritual endeavors seem to be outrageous anyway.

People mention the God Thing somewhat reluctantly. But like a compulsion it gets expression. The effect is cathartic and energizing. It brings on such excitement and motivation, such a release of energy. We will bring people to God, in the Indian Way! Singing and dancing the Indian way, was praying! Dinners and give-aways, sharing and caring, was praying! Activities conducted in the sweat-houses, were praying! Showing reverence to the Land or Mother Earth, was praying!

Praying, we are all convinced leads to the necessary changes. There was solid reality in our approach that guaranteed some success. One transformation success would be a priceless accomplishment!

Such faith! The initial euphoria is balanced by a honest look at the reality of the situation confronting us. Supposedly better people have tried and failed.   All of us have come through a life crisis or catastrophe with more strength and vitality, being truly transformed.   Catastrophes and tragedies presented the participants the path to healing.   Appreciation for life comes from the nearness to disaster and an intimate awareness of one's own mortality.   Pain and suffering contrast the peace and comfort we experience within ourselves now, as opposed to the insanity of our prior existence. We all know that "it took what it took", for us to get where we are at now. And where we are at now seems to be where God intended us to be.

I always envisioned finding "salvation" meant becoming a convert, and it was viewed as a loss rather than a change for the better. I have since come to learn that it means to heal. Another misunderstood term is "repent", all that it means is to re-think, change one's mind, or to think differently.   So one of our problems is to overcome the stigma of the language attached to spiritual endeavor. So we need to find a process that will help our people think in new ways about healing the wounds that have built up over generations.

What we have achieved through enormous struggle, we strive to instill in others by communication and sharing, in effect being the messengers of good news. Let's get them to know the comfort, the peace and serenity, that comes from being true to the Self. If we sit still long enough to examine intimately the pain and suffering, if we don't anesthetize ourselves, comes the salvation and repentance of recognizing our real selves.

In the deepest despair or hopelessness, one must search through the darkness, coldness, and emptiness of a suffering heart. After the rage and self pity disappate, one must wander though the wreckage of personal turmoil and tormented history. Through this process one comes face to face to with one's self, and an encounter with one's God. Rebirth and transformation are the hallmarks of such encounters. Hope and strength are the currency of those who come through such experience alive and growing. Where previously the helpful hopefuls and the strong, were viewed as intrusive busy-bodies, now comes the understanding of their desperate need to help.

The safety man came to, through the teachings of a twelve-step, self-help program. The social worker and the computer programmer came through the Seven Drums Religion, and related similar twelve-step programs. The policeman and the housing guy were born again Christians, devout Catholics, actually they were leaders in the local reservation Cursillo Movement. Most of the people present were deeply effected by the Cursillo Movement.

None of the group are zealous in their spirituality. But all of us are searching for deeper meanings for what we've been through. "I thank the Maker for being still alive. I thank the Maker for still having the ability to feel and know. I thank the Maker for the survival techniques that come from deep within our genetic make-up. In my gratitude I recognize that I'm truly blessed...", the group, a fellowship of survivors, is bent on helping others survive, showing those still suffering a cleaner path to enlightenment.

Manifest Destiny Visited on the Colville

In Washington State History, a required course that I took in Coulee Dam High School in 1966, there was no mention of the Colville Indian Reservation. Indians are mentioned in passing, nothing sigficant. It so happened that the Indians gave up a significant and sizable portion of North Central Washington, in exchange for rights to live into perpetuity on this reserve. No one mentions that the reservation is one seventh of its original size, the other six parts were appropriated for the Washingtonians. Less than two years after the first agreement was reached with the various bands to go to live on the original reservation, the U. S. Government nullified the agreement. A new one was made up, which allocated the Moses Allotment, some estimated four million acres, to farmers, ranchers, and miners in the Methow, Entiat, and Chelan valleys and mountain ranges. Shortly thereafter the North Half was "returned to the public domain", this was about 1.5 million acres. In the meantime the Colville area for which the reservation is named, was somehow disappeared, this portion alone comprised about 25% of the original reservation. These areas make up what is now known as Chelan, Okanagon, Ferry, and Stevens Counties of Washington State. Never even got kissed before we were screwed.

The Congress and the Government of the United States claims there is a special relationship between the U.S.A. and Indian. The only thing special is the grand scale of the fraud, and swindling carried out under the guise of legality. A map of the current reservation will reveal a checkboard pattern of ownership for he Colville Confederated Tribes. Apparently the previous acquistions for the white people weren't enough, the reservation was opened for homesteading. It was treated as if there were no people here. We're surrounded by towns and people proud of their pioneer heritage, they are blind to the fact that their heritage is founded on duplicity and deception.

The Columbia River runs along the eastern and southern borders of the current reservation. Kettle Falls was a major crossroad of commerce and cultural exchange long before there were any white people in this area. It was a major source of salmon, since the falls provided a means for the Indians to come and get a winter supply. They could either catch or trade to fill their need. The San Poil was another major salmon fishery. The Methow, Wenatchee, Okanagon, and Entiat rivers were salmon fisheries, inhabited by the bands that were to be moved to the reservation. I can still remember going up the Chewack River, which is a tributary to the Methow River, and spearing the spring run Chinook.

The San Poil and Kettle Falls fisheries are just a fading memory, lying underneath the surface of Lake Roosevelt. In the first half of this century the Columbia was harnessed for electrical power generation. The Grand Coulee and Chief Joseph Dams, proud achievements of the White Guys, disappeared the salmon right before our very eyes. Half of the cradle of the salmon was obliterated. Many held a vigil to watch Kettle Falls sink from their sight forever. Some salmon seem to carry memories of spawning grounds above the these two dams, because they keep trying to migrate past the Chief Joseph Dam.

There is a dispute among the White Guys now, they are fighting over whether or not the dams on the Columbia have eliminated the salmon. When I can't see Kettle Falls, or say, Celilo Falls, I would have to conclude that the dams are the blame. The White Guys see it differently, they must have a peculiar set of eyeballs. In a society of a variety of competing needs, there is no room to be honest about the cause of the salmon's demise. When a person kills another person and displays no ill effects on his or her conscience, society calls them socio-pathic. When a person has no regard for reality they're either insane or just outright liars. The salmon was very much a person killed by a socio-path, there certainly has been absolutely no remorse about its destruction. Nuts to the idea that the dams have had nothing to do with the drastic decline in the salmon population.

The bands on the Colville Indian Reservation were heavily dependant on salmon, it provided the bulk of their sustenance. The cycles and seasons for culture followed that of the salmon. The salmon was revered and honored, because of its life-giving sustenance it was considered sacred. When the salmon were stopped by the dams, a deadly blow to the Indians' soul was administered, a very powerful bad medicine. The dams dried up something intrinsic to the Indian heart, only slowly are we beginning to realize the extent of the disaster. It has taken sixty years for the shock to wear off, and to realize that which not only sustained our bodies but our souls, disappeared along with the Kettle Falls.

When white society thinks about the Indian problem, they ponder psychological, political, and economic solutions. In the recovery and healing of souls, mankind has always recognized the process as spiritual. The problem is that neither the victims or perpetrators can comprehend the enormity of this sin against the earth and its people.

The scientific approach underlying the problem solving methodology, hasn't developed the scope to comprehend the implications of not only the demise of the Wanapums, but of the Salmon Tribe, the Wolf Tribe, the Grizzly Tribe. They have not even addressed the issue with enough regard for reality, to determine whether the demise was a natural evolutionary process or not.

Manifest Destiny still marches on. Its tradition may well be implemented by some of the survivors. Just mention of traditional Indian values to those in power in Indian governments. Although many give it lip service, most view it with suspicion. Rather than examine the values, an argument over what is more Indian or more "traditional", ensues.

This is the heritage of Manifest Destiny. We are divided, arguing and squabbling amongst ourselves, savengers fighting over a carcass. The establishment or controlling group of Indians is smaller than those sitting on the edge of destruction. And while these people sitting on the edge die, the establishment argues over it public image. This is a perfect example of a low regard for reality, and an emphasis on public relations.

Circling Closer - Finding the Itch

Coming to terms with the source of our problems is a difficult task. It requires much exeperience in life as an Indian. It requires acceptance of some rather difficult facts about life. And when the answer seems to have been found, we discover it has moved off, further on the horizon, much like the rainbow. But most of all it requires being able to see reality as it is, this requires much honesty.

There is something that irritates our complacency, and demands that we attend to it. It is much like an itch that won't be ignored.

When most people reach that age when it is time to rush to meet life with zest, and say yes to all of the possibilities, we seem to be running down. Many of our young Indians have not yet asked life's most compelling fundamental questions. "Why am I here?" "Who am I?" A life without direction or purpose leads to the despair and hopelessness. This condition leads to questions like - "Why should I live", "Why should I keep on trying?". The tremendous highs that come from booze and drugs cannot compensate for the eventual depressions. The confusion and disillusionment without letup or resolution, kills the vision of any hope in their young hearts. "But by the goodness of the Creator", we managed to continue existing in the here and now.

By the grace of the Creator, we search for the reason and motivation why many are still aggressively seeking the life the leads to despair. If everyone can see the results of that way of living, by what compelling reason should they pursue it? We can only conclude from our own experience that it was to escape. It also seems that we were trying to escape from the very place that is to be our eventual destination. Which, is our very selves. We started out in a very bad place to begin with, and along the way, we forgot the blessings.

What could erase from our inherent memories and natural

grace, the concept that we were made in the image and likeness of the Creator, that this was our true heritage? This personal truth necessitates a very rigorous program to educate a person to believe otherwise. The Creator brought us into existence in purity. The Creator brought us into existence to be good enough to meet any challenge. The Creator brought us into existence as beings filled with innocence, with beauty, with awesome potential. The Creator blessed us with gifts that would allow us to achieve and accomplish grandly. The Creator instilled in us a reverence for life, a belief that nature was sacred and holy.

The Indian, despite all of the Creator's blessings, is taught from early on in life, that he was born into the wrong race. Being he was born, not by his choice, into the wrong race, it was a sin he would spend his life trying to rectify. So early on, begins the rigorous program to erase his or her personal sense of rightness and grace. Early on, begins the rigorous program to erase knowledge of the Creator's blessings, whose effects only a miracle will change. The program is institutionalized in the mass media, entertainment, education, religion, in civic gatherings, every facet of American culture.

This program has eliminated from much of our thinking that there is a spiritual realm, from which the life we see, springs forth. The Mother has become the great outdoors - nature, a source of resources to exploit. Hunters go out now and kill, there is no remorse or concern over killing a living thing. The reverence for life has dissappeared. Gratitude for the bountiful creation is an alien concept. The spiritual powers of the animals has been transformed into fetishes and superstition. The mountains and forests are places we go to, rather than be part of. We are separate from the land, a living breathing entity, that is no longer integral to our being. Some of us are convinced that the mountains and forests are dangerous for us. We are White Men Indians with our great concern over our lawns and shrubs. The sacred nature of water is forgotten in our haste to irrigate and keep these lawns green.

Half of our people have surrendored to what greater America calls Indian social ills. They have not only indulged in alcohol, drugs, and violence, but use these to replace the usual Indian values that give meaning to life. The poverty that plagues our people is not only economical but spiritual. We have allowed ourselves to become dependant on handouts. We have allowed ourselves to become the visual evidence of a successful indoctrination of inferiority. We ourselve, now by our own example, give the visual justification for the attitudes of prevailing society.

We look back at our ancestors. We look at the lands where they roamed and made their living. And we experience a longing and a need. But we haven't the slightest clue as to what it is we crave. All we know is that we are constantly reminded that those beautiful lands are no longer part of us. We are part of the mountains and rivers conquered by the pioneering efforts of the Americans.

How is it that we have acquired the values to pursue things in life? Our young people and ourselves, want fast cars, computers, entertainment systems, money. Everything we chase in life has to do with our image we want to project to others. What other people think of us is more important that what we think about ourselves. Where is the source of self-worth and self-respect? The source of values that kept our people healthy and alive for eons has dried up. So now we zip along on a fast road to self- destruction.

How is it that we are so gullible? Why do we have to smell good, like pine or lemons? Why have bright teeth? Why be like Mike? Don't we have any inner messages that tell us the life-giving truths? Why have we tuned out our information from our higher selves? Why can't we form our own ideas about who we are and what should be important to us?

Many of our unfortunate people are completely unaware that there is a higher self. We have starved this higher self which thrives on spiritual sustenance. Some of us who look for this inner voice, find it very faint and weak. Again we can look to the culture we live in, the mass media, education, religion, government, all tell us who we are. We believe and reinforce the image we have of ourselves.

We carry shame because we are told we are a defeated people. Why should we carry shame when compassion and generousity compelled us to help the newcomers? When peaceful people are simply overwhelmed, why claim glory and superiority in this? And who is always telling us these facts of life? Why is it repeated endlessly, in an endless variety of ways?

We were overwhelmed because we new that we didn't own the air and sky; that we didn't own the rivers like the ones that gave us our salmon. The ground we walked on, we shared with the deer, bear, and all our other brothers. The ground that gave us our food and water, we didn't own. These were gifts from the Creator, to be shared with all our brothers of the Earth.

The majority of our people are becoming adherents to the belief in the almighty dollar. These are the "Good Indians", but they don't fit the stereotypical pattern of Indians. Like most of America, they are chasing after status and prestige, financial security, and more of this and that. What they don't recognize is that they end up with more wanting of things that don't fulfill basic needs. They gain things that aren't life giving. Many of our people here look at the other half and wonder if they are having more fun. Fun, being entertained and distracted, are the driving forces of local society.

The campaign for Manifest Destiny has been a success. We are assimilated almost totally into mainstream society. We try to fit in. We dress and shower, to make sure we smell clean. We go to church on Sunday to appear as righteous citizens. We operate highly efficient bureaucracies. Our people now are part of that frenetic activity to acquire more, to exploit, to compete. We teach our children to be patriotic, and to love America. And America condescends to put up with our presence.

Condescension is what damages the human spirit. Even more damaging is our own insistance on playing the role of the victim. The answer to our problems lie in the nature of the problem. The nature of the problem is the dominant society's inhumanity to an oppressed minority sector of society. And we the oppressed don't know anything else but being the victim.

Is it conceivable that we could change this pardigm? Is this talk of the necessity of a miracle overstating the problem?

It is highly unlikely. Two things will happen if we don't make an effort. One, we will be totally assimilated into the dominant American culture, convinced we are second class citizens, and treated as such. Two, we will continue dying from our own excesses, until we are no more.

Each one of us resents the indoctrination of inferiority foisted on us by society at large. We resent it but we don't make any effort to change it. We have resigned to the belief that this is the way it will always be. This is the education program that destroys our people. It indoctrinated Indians into believing they are less than the non-Indian, less in worthiness, less in capability, less in humanity. And now we are incapacitated, we can't act, we can't feel, we are stuck in rock hard apathy.

Propagation of the American Myth

It was immensely satisfying seeing Dances With Wolves, and seeing that the actors playing many of the central figures in the plot, were Indians. No one seems to notice however that the tribe in that movie didn't have any reality to non-Indian society, until a white man and a white woman came into their lives. Much of the Indian reality is treated pretty much the same way.

The movies play a large part in the enculturation of the American people. If anything is significant about American culture, it is that it was propagated throughout the world through the movies, cartoons, and the mass media. Thus the America cultural attitude towards Indians is a Hollywood attitude. At one time it seemed necessary to boost American morale during the Great Depression and the War Years. They created and sustained the American Myth of the rugged individual, - ambitious hard working, optimistic and motivated, - pioneering, - scientific. Somehow his destiny - to conquer the wilderness and the Indian.

Myths are the means for cultures to teach the young to be successful in their societies. It is how they teach their young about who they are at the most basic and fundamental level. Strong, if not stronger than any truths, these myths. The American Myth is particularly devastating to Indians.

The American Myth is about White American superiority. The American Myth is also about Indian inferiority. And because we have all become believers in the new religion of "Science", somehow the myth was correlated with science. It is the new religion, science with all its authority and seemingly immutable laws.

The anthropologists call these types of myths, ethnocentric, and pretty much a universal phenomenon. So it is likely that the Indian Myth featured Indian superiority. The problem now is that we are Indians in the American Culture, subjected to the myths of that culture. So as Indians, we become enculturated into becoming inferior to white people.

To a very great extent, the dream or vision America has for the Indian, has largely come to pass. Through a campaign of distortion or outright lies, the spirit and heart of the Indians peoples have been seriously wounded. We have always recovered from the misfortunes of war. Can we rebound from an indoctrination of inferiority? We will face formidable challenges from a society that has a mania for bigotry and racism disguised as entertainment and enculturation.

Children during play reinforce the myths. As child in play, I was always a good Indian, I died many times in conflicts with the cowboys. The good guys were always the cowboys or the cavalry, the bad guys were Indians. This model for play acting would, in my own mind, cause me to stereotype myself for life. Even in real life there exists a bleak destiny for Indians. Bad guys were always in for a bad ending. Achievements and accomplishment would never occur for the bad guys. So to survive, I felt it necessary to become a good guy.

Becoming a good guy meant denying my own intrinsic worth. I value the light skin, the blue eyes, wavy hair. My standard of acceptable beauty is not Indian. Non-Indians are assumed to be smarter, more competent. I confuse loudness and being vocal with intelligence, and I imitate. I become embarrassed at my own color, and racial characteristics, and the embarrassment becomes shame.

The movie "Dances With Wolves" was precedent setting because Indian actors portrayed Indians relating to each other and various situations in life. Before this occurrence, it was rare that an Indian would play a major role in any movie. If a central figure was an Indian, a non-Indian would play it. This went a long way towards telling Indians subliminally what was acceptable to society about Indians. Society certainly didn't understand Indians, because all the portrayals of Indian characters were shallow and stupid. That is probably the only way society would accept developing our own view of Indians.

In one of the most popular novels of American literature, the "Last of the Mohicans", the author can't relate it to his audience until he includes a non-Indian into the plot. Later on many novels have a blond, blue-eyed non-Indian, becoming part of a tribe, and then becoming chief. Indians aren't going to have decent leadership unless some non-Indian comes in and shows them how.

In the movies, non-Indians are always portrayed as coming into a tribe and winning the heart of the most beautiful woman. This woman is always the daughter of a powerful chief, who for some inexplicable reason is just proud as hell to have a white-man son-in-law. Of course this beautiful woman is portrayed by a non-Indian with dark make-up. It should be noted that the relationships portrayed is always of one between the non-Indian man and the Indian woman, who for some reason, always ends up dying for the guy. It should be no mystery then that the first acceptable portrayal of an Indian by an Indian in a major movie role, was in "One Flew Over the Cuckoos Nest". The situation of this charactor in this movie, is representative of the situation of all Indians. Society has put us somewhere, out of the way, so they don't have to deal with us.

The true renditions of Indians in art by the non-Indian establishment, have been givus us by Remington and Russell. Somehow that tradition hasn't been upheld. They have done the same thing they have done to acquire a blond wavy haired, blue eyed Jesus Christ.

Even in the arts, society only accepts the portrayal of the Indian as an inferior doomed to be defeated.

Youngsters instinctively model themselves after winners, and the winners always seemed to be the good guys. The losers were the bad guys so that path was never attractive. There wasn't something or someone to correct the misconception that Indians were the bad guys. The bad guys were losers, the losers were Indians, so the Indians are the bad guys. So who are the models for Indian youngsters to emulate?

What has caused the most terrific damage has been the portrayal of the medicine man or shaman. Most Indians had a number of leaders who had responsibility for certain aspects of Indian life. The medicine man had responsibility for the spiritual and ceremonial life. The Hollywood propaganda machine portrays the shaman as a primitive, bumbling clown, easily discounted as a worshipper of something less than the divine. At the very least, he is sadly mislead by his beliefs. Where as the war chief was given tidbits and scraps of respect, the shaman was relegated to the object of derision, impotent in the face of the superior non-Indian, and the new religion of science. The healer probably was the first and biggest loser in this indoctrination of inferiority. Indirectly, we are the big losers, an alternative to shame and degradation, the loss of our spirituality, was booze, drugs, and violence.

The shaman was portrayed as a sham. The very word is leaden with meaning derogatory to the healer. Today, many Indians believe he is a farce, and his practices childish. In the shaman, Hollywood, in the most demeaning fashion, caricturized Indian Culture as cartoonish. Eventually we were indoctrinated. We thought he delved in superstition and preyed on the fears of the ignorant through magicians' trickery. The dancing, praying and sacred ceremonies were never portrayed honestly. Being mesmerized by the propaganda of the myth-makers we, as youngsters, deserted the spiritual ways of our people.

Men and women of Indian spiritual substance survived, and their practices, however arcane to the "now" Indian. In my way I will try to honor these "good guys".

Touching The Raw Nerve

Indians had no significance to the American psyche until they became an obstacle to the American Way. First, there were the Eastern Tribes and as Manifest Destiny unfolded, the Western Tribes. None receives mention as having anything significant to do with American history. It is as if prior to contact with non-Indians the inhabitants of the continent had not any independent reality.

When I first heard the real history of the treatment of Indians by the non-Indians, I was greatly shocked. This is a testament to the amount of the non-Indian American Culture I had assimilated. The enculturation via the communication from education, civic involvement, religion, mass media, entertainment, society in general, made me think and act, like I wasn't what I was, an Indian. I rooted for the good guys in the movies, or the horse operas on T.V., the heroes of Louis L'Amore or Zane Grey.

I have to think that non-Indians must deny the history between Indians and non-Indians ever happened. These people couldn't done such terrible things, because "these" people were my people, since I was so thoroughly American.

I knew about the violation of treaties, but somehow there just had to be mitigating circumstances. Didn't they teach us that this was done in the name of progress? Good guys just didn't act that way. All of what took place couldn't have been motivated by greed and deception. There certainly was no place for genocide or destruction of entire cultures, that was something for Hitler's Germany. Anyway the treaty concept made for a romantic story-line, that was what we had become, a part in a storyline. It was part and parcel of the American Myth. And as with many myths you can take some liberties with the facts of the matter.

Very much like victims of abuse, I became strongly identified with the abuser, and denied the true nature of abuses. I had become totally American, albeit a second or third class American. But this didn't mean I was accepted as an American by the non-Indians. If I was accepted, I had to compromise, and accept the second and third class treatment. The way I was naturally, just was not acceptable. This was the first intimation that a terrible void existed within me, something was missing. I think this happens to all Indians, a creeping disillusionment. A person of Indian descent starts to recognize that he is treated different. "You can have the American Dream, but the good parts are reserved for non-Indians."

Each one of us has been told and taught that some how we are less worthy and less valuable than the non-Indian. This becomes internalized and intrinsic to our nature, when this happens, we end up with a sickness or dis-ease, rooted in our very soul.

When I went to high-school I was removed from an algebra class and sent to a general math class. This was done rather arbitrarily to make room for a non-Indian, since the class was filled up. I was removed from a biology class and sent to a general science class, again to make room in the biology class. This seems to have been done matter of factly, without any hostility or overt bigotry. But this was one of the first times I had recognized that I had received a terrible insult to my dignity and self-respect. I became aware that my education wasn't as important as the people for whom I had to make room. This has always been the Indian's plight, making room for somebody else.

What makes this so objectionable is that this type of treatment of Indians was not only accepted but expected by society at large. The students who benefited from my removal were shown that their particular needs were superior to the Indians concerns. Indian ambition and assertiveness received crushing blows early in life. Later on in life, non-Indians automatically expected their needs would always be paramount relative to the Indians.

Kids will fight, it is a given. In high school if you fought with another Indian, the authorities thought, hey, that's the way Indians are. If you fought a white boy, and you lost, hey, that's the way Indians are. If you fought a white boy, and won, you were in violation of the Myth, and the laws the dominant society were enforced against you. If it was a situation where you defended yourself, both the perpetrator and you were punished.

There was an individual who showed up at a general meeting of the Tribal membership, he looked pretty awful and pathetic. He was in and out of prison, was a drunk, and a drug user. He pointed out his situation to the establishment. "Look what happened to me when I tried to become a White Man. I've tried the white man's schools, the white man's jobs, the white man's prisons, the booze, the drugs, and I'm lucky to be alive. I don't make a very good white man. We need something that will help Indians like me. Not some more white man's programs"

The State of Minds

A Japanese comedian gave me the first hint about this phenomena of the American Myth. This comedian did an imitation of John Wayne, and I noticed that some of the audience didn't find that funny. I had heard Indians make reference to John Wayne as a metephore for the treatment of ethnic minorities by White people. I could feel and understand much about what was expressed and felt, by this comedian, and probably more about what wasn't expressed. Those that didn't find the comedian funny, probably felt this also. I could identify with someone else's experience, such as this comedian, with racial discrimination and oppression. I finally started hearing and asking the question myself, "Why put up with this?"

John Wayne is the embodiment of the American Myth. This was the myth that was the blue-print for turning out the Americans. After a while, he doesn't even have to be John Wayne, any white guy would do. John Wayne never single handedly, on the righteous side of justice and the American Way, slaughtered or gunned down hundreds of New Yorkers, Kentuckians, or Texans. That would run completely counter to the American truth. John Wayne heroically defended the American Way from "Nips", "Krauts", "Gooks", "Ivan", and the "Hun", all sorts of generally sub-human groups. But by far the group he is mostly identified with in fighting, was the "Redskins" or "Savages". The Duke, the American Cowboy, or the trusty Calvary, if he wasn't cuffing Indians up along side the head for their own good, he was gunning them down, like the supply would never run out.

In the current trend, the American Myth is starting to develop clay feet so to speak. American superiority in technology and business is faced with serious challenges from the Japan. You might say this is causing disruptions of mythical proportions. So part of the American Myth has to change. All that is left to be superior to, is the Indians.

This is proving easier to maintain because a lot Indians believe in the American Myth. As was mentioned earlier, the victims are identifying with the offender. You would never get them to admit to someone else's superiority, but they do fall into the habit of feeling inferior. It starts with the young being separated from their parents and loved ones. The young are turned over to whomever society confers the sacred trust to nurture the young, be it school teachers, principles, bureaucrats, local city and county officials, preachers, policeman, politicians, entertainers, and media people. These are the people vested with authority of moral superiority, the backing of technology, and the scientific method. Whether it is their intention or not, they invariably isolate an Indian youth and start the conditioning process of indoctrination. All I have to do is remember and I'm there, like many of our youth, even today. These people always manage to program you, condition you to think and believe there is something wrong with you. Stand before each of them to be judged and be told what your shortcomings are, "Keep your hands to yourself, - (with an air of superiority) I hope you can understand such a simple idea, - (with an expression of repugnance) lets some fresh air into the room, - (with all the self-righteous indignation they can muster) don't you lie to me, don't be looking at our young ladies, - when will you learn? - Why can't you people be like the rest of us?" Get the repetitions in, then you begin to accept tidbits of what they tell you, -finally total agreement.

If there is anything consistent about relating to the non-Indian, it is the humiliation and degradation. In the Indian was cultivated the sense of his or her own unworthiness. On an almost ritual basis was the indoctrination of inferiority. This was the idea that because you are an Indian you are not good as the non-Indian. People think that this is a thing of the past.

The result is a compulsiveness to seek approval from figures of authority, in one extreme, to violent rebellion in the other. One aspect is to be obsessively trying to prove yourself good enough. Working twice as hard to prove you deserve half the wages non-Indians make. Not allowing yourself to be yourself, to be acceptable. It is a trap almost all Indians fall into, and many don't make their way out.

Each of us fall into the role of the stoic, sullen or noble savage, in dealing with non-Indians. This sounds better than mumbling, bumbling, stumbling incoherently. All someone had to do was present a front of superiority, condescension or patronization, - and it happened. It is a trigger for me to resort to my conditioned role. The effect is like a post-hypnotic suggestion. In my case, it used to happen before I could even try to react differently.

In each of our own mind's visioning process is the repetitive movie or script depicting Indians wildly charging off to self destruction. Much of this script has been the result of different movies and television series playing the same scene in a repetitive loop. Repetition is the key, because the vision programs us. And unconsciously, in some mad fashion we correlate the vision with reality, to mean that our role was one of self destruction.

In recalling some of my past behavior, I felt like I was cast in a very unsatisfying role. It was not a role of choice. It is a role that has evolved into one of an arhcetypal nature. It is a role in a paradigm America reserves for the Indian. We need to make a conscious choice in the roles we act out in society. The model imposed on us is dysfunctional, and the powers that be, seem to want to keep it that way. As various people keyed my behavior I responded with the appropriate programmed reactions. There is a sense of futility, when one realizes that all one gets to do in life is react. When a people just wait for the next stimulus, to activate the next response, there results a sense of demoralization,

Is there some other script, image, or role we revert to, when interrelating to non-Indians? The sense of powerlessness or impotence makes an individual feel that all that is left available to them, is a last resort. The last resort is violent defiance and reckless behavior. This role is also used by non-Indians, the warrior myth of going out in a blaze of glory, "Hail to Valhalla!" The law enforcement agencies refer to these incidents, as "Suicide by cop".

Another role is the solitary man or woman, totally indifferent to surroundings and people. This may not be a role. So much pain, have turned many to anaesthetize themselves in alcohol and drugs. With these, many of our people sentence themselves to solitary confinement, and isolation, even in a crowd of people.

While we are examining these various phenomena, we have to address some fundamental human needs. We have the desire to be accepted by our fellows. We have a desire and need to have a sense of belonging. We have a desire and need to belong to a group where we fit it, where there is some homogeneity. Indians for our efforts, we are made to stick out like a cold sore. We are made so aware of our differences that somehow are conferred as inferior. The self awareness or to be more exact, this self consciosness, is as much Indian, as the color of our skin.

We somehow have acquired the false belief, that to be someone different than from our real selves, is the key to acceptance from our fellows. Some how the effect of this stereotyping of Indians has created a conviction that to be real is unacceptable. So we have people distorting their sense of self. We have people perverting their sense of self worth to belong. The feeling of worthlessness and powerlessness underlies much of the mayhem in our Indian society.

Are we so unacceptable because we are a bunch of drunken, lazy, violent people? Or are we a bunch of drunken, lazy, violent people because we find ourselve unaccepted, the way we naturally are? It does't matter to mainstream society, because the Indians are held accountable. It doesn't matter that we are recovering from the destruction of what makes a people a community or a society. In this mode of living, the sense of reality is very tenuous.

Are we mystified or are we under a magic spell to keep us in this frame of mind? I don't even know if the word usage is correct. But now the term sticks in my mind. We automatically slip into survival mode of surreality or detachment, when confronted with racism. Our responses and reactions as the result of operant conditioning, have created some extremely strong habits. And like a subject of the hypnotist, a snap of the finger and we revert to form.

Is this the archetype or paradigm of a defeated people? There is a good possibility that this is the case. Society dictates what is expected of us in our interaction with the non-Indian. Much of this craziness makes for much difficulty in dealing with the source of the problem. Do we address the bad habits we have developed? Or do we address the bad way society looks down upon us? Are our problems so different that the obvious solutions are the wrong solutions?

It is worthwhile examining ourselves for the solution of our dilemmas. We need to ask ourselves some critical questions about our values and beliefs, that so far we've taken for granted. It should be obvious by now that some of these unexamined values and beliefs are not foundations to stand on, but shackles that imprison us.

Years of habitual thinking, brought about by the indoctrination of inferiority, have to be eliminated. The return to sanity starts in our own heads. The acceptance and love, begins with acceptance and compassion towards ourselves. The source of what is real in life is to surrender to powers found within each of us.

This Can't Happen Among Our Own!

The worst damage has been to our system of values and beliefs. Our morality seems to have been seriously eroded among our spiritual and political leadership. The manifestation of this situation is the way the establishment on the reservation treats Indians.

The problem of abusing Indian people is not limited to the non-Indian. Within our own tribe there are people who treat fellow tribal members as inferiors. Again this may be the product of the indoctrination, but also of spiritual deprivation. Without the development of self worth, or any healthy concept of self, the higher order functions of personality and character suffer.

There is a cadre of people who are not full blood or not dark skinned Indians. Because they are lighter skinned they have presumed themselves to be more adept at leading the Tribe, and there are many dark-skinned Indians who believe them.

The current situation can only have come about as the result of the indoctrination of inferiority. The voters assume there is a correlation between light skin and intelligence, or with capability in leading. They presume the lighter skinned people who have the non-Indian characteristics and behavior patterns, as having superior qualifications. The lighter skinned tribal members take advantage of this perception. Some will adopt the condescension, the patronization, and even the superior attitude towards the darker skinned tribal members. Because of the enculturation of inferiority, the darker tribal members fall into the role of the "inferior", because the lighter skinned tribal members can key that behavior with their own actions. The indoctrination of inferiority conditions the darker skinned Indians into behaving inferior.

There is the sad example of an individual's inability to articulate their concerns in English. This person struggles to come up with the words to describe feelings and ideas. Someone who speaks English real well will finish the statements and sentences for this person. In some cases the person struggling will be ridiculed, at the very least, be the focus of some very patronizing assistance.

There are Indians here who will even treat the spirituality practiced before Christrianity arrived, with the same sanctimonious and self righteous contempt of a fire and brimstone preacher or evangilist. The very activities that should help our people most are vehicles for the indoctrination of inferiority.

The lighter skinned Indians have adopted the practices of a very authoritarian approach, in dealing with the dark skinned Indians. Again this approach appears to have the backing of technology and the scientific methodology already proven successful, that gives the appearance of validity. This is the way they practice the methods that key or trigger the sense of inferiority.

This conditioning extends to the voters who seem inclined to view the lighter skinned individuals as more competent to lead. I would have to believe this is the condition in some of the reservation districts who repeatedly elect lighter skinned individuals, even when there is a preponderance of dark skinned tribal members in that district.

These people seem to strive to perpetuate the American Myth against the darker tribal members. The employment is a good example. Statistically there should be more Indian managers and administrators, but there aren't. There are people educated and experienced enough, but they are the dark skinned Indians. When there exists the condition between selecting between the lighter skinned tribal member and the dark skinned one, the lighter skinned tribal member invariably prevails. It has nothing to do with qualifications, but that there exists an unwritten double standard. If you're dark skinned and educated, you automatically lack experience, or are deemed a trouble maker.

In our tribal government organization there exists a thing called the Inter-disciplinary Team. They heavily influence the management of our natural resources. On this team there are no economists, financial managers, no anthropologists, no sociologists, no native healers, no cultural specialists. But there are geologists, foresters, hydrologists, silviculturists, soil specialists, botanists, ecologist, environmentalists, and fish and game biologists. All disciplines that are authoritarian and have the apparent support of technology and science. These disciplines emphasize exploiting the environment. This team keeps Indians at bay in the name of good management practices. Fifty per-cent of our tribal payroll goes to twenty-five percent of the workforce, who are non-Indian.

If one were to look at the people in the pinnacle or key positions of our government, one would discover that few if any merit their positions. This is, at least with regard to accomplishment and achievement in a sense that furthers the living standard of our people. There is always the rhetoric of educating our people, but once a person is educated, the political establishement and bureacracy treat this person as a pariah.

If one were to look at the ideals of these people, there is striking absence of integrity. Moral courage is never the basis of any decision arrived at through this leadership. They have a standard for integrity that seems to be, what is expedient, as opposed to what is the right thing to do. A look at those considered successful, one would see a person very ruthless in dealing with people who demand things like justice and fairness for our people. This is in contrast to traditional leadership who put the band or the tribe's well being first over personal needs.

But as with most democracies, the leadership reflects the highest values of the constituency. The responsibility for the leadership we have lies with the voters. And once again we come face to face with apathy and cynicism.

In any organization information is a strategic resource. The management of natural resources involves processing data and information about the trees, land, water, minerals, animals, air quality, plants, insects, the conditions of these, the location, the value, the costs, and volumes. Never the actual objects, but data surrogates. There are no Indians managing information, by a conscious choice they are screened from that involvement. The

Indians who are the managers in the areas of natural resource, finance, or any other area critical to functional management are not educated in the disciplines to manage them. They hire non-Indian professional staffs to do it. The result is another barrier to Indian progress, because these so called Indian managers protect the non-Indian positions, to protect their own.

The establishment has a prescription for what they call progress. The Indians need more education; they need more management training; they need more experience; they need more self esteem; they need more professionalism; they need to make themselves better. What they are telling the Indian people, "You have to make yourselves like the white people". The problem is, that while the Indian is making himself more like a white person, the establishment and the non-Indians will still treat the Indian as inferior, and the Indian will still believe them.

When Indians work many of them quit because they are required to compromise their dignity and self-respect in some fashion. Many of them have very little to begin with, but they are expected to surrender the last least bit they have. If you want to thin out the Indian employees, get arrogant or overbearing, they'll quit showing up for work, those lazy bums.

One thing we can learn from the Japanese experience is that they made the management disciplines and the scientific method a positive force for their cultural values and beliefs. They applied principles taken from American management and applied Japanese strengths inherent to the people. This created the business environment that emphasized their cultural uniqueness.

This should be remembered when employers complain that they can't get enough Indian workers so they have to hire non-Indians. They create the atmosphere that denigrates Indians.

There is a reasoning that defies logic when the established politicians and administrators are confronted with this phenomena. Their arbitrary rebuttal is, "There can't racism and discrimination because we're all Indians." Denial? Denial! Denial.

There is this ranking occurring where the dark skinned Indians are relegated to the bottom of the pecking order. I think society decides who are Indians and who are acceptable non-Indian look alikes. To maintain their positions the non-Indian look alikes maintain the indoctrination of inferiority.

There have been people who have sought to make changes in this area, but for whatever reason they are coerced into changing their stance, or frustrated into quitting. Power and its uses are perverted in our system. One thing is encouraging, people who have been branded as trouble makers, are appealing to a larger and larger portion of tribal members. The politics of this arena aren't sophisticated enough as of yet to enlighten the constituency to the power they misuse out of ignorance and non-use. Indians have to awaken to the results of their own apathy, because the ability to make choices may atrophy.

We Don't Even Know What We Lost!

There is a sense of frustration in the feeling that we don't know what we lost. There is something missing in all of us who were victimized by racism. The sense of loss as has been characterized, claims Indians have no self worth or self esteem. Many Indians are frustrated by loss of identity, or loss of cultural attachment. It may go much deeper than that. It could be the loss of our very selves, the ability to act and feel as human beings.

Somewhere along the way we lost the sense of grace about ourselves. We lost the valuation and validation from within ourselves. The sense of rightness of our being, simply because we existed, was severed from our consciousness. Without this sense we seek our valuation and validation from an external source, not from a god or within ourselves, but from other people. And these other people don't want us to have a healthy view of the self.

Losses create emptiness and nothingness. There exists within us, spiritual vacuums that aren't being filled. We have woundedness that is not being healed, we have these lingering losses.

The losses of lands, water, and the usual hunting, fishing, and gathering places are the most evident and painful. We have even witnessed the land and rivers change in their purpose and use. There are other losses that we are only beginning to comprehend.

At the root of many of our losses is the story of our people. We have lost the roots of our culture. We have lost the continuity enjoyed by the rest of the American culture. Where are the legendary heroes to aspire to, after which our young people can model themselves? Where are to stories of heroism and achievement? Most of these have been lost with our language, and with our ceremonies.

Many people can look at societies sources of wisdom and find their beginnings. Somehow I don't feel that ours were those identified with 1776. Finding the real course of events that brought us to this point in our existance, is certainly going to cause some difficulties. The making of the information public to our people, is likely to be discouraged.

The trails and paths back to our roots will give us the fundamental values and beliefs that will guide us. What has guided us in the last one hundred years as our culture was dismantled? We have fragments. We have parts of ceremonies, and remnants of songs. We are missing purposes for many of these remnants. Like Coyote's Song, there are only hints of the great beauty that was lost.

In 1988, I can remember struggling to hold back tears brought about by some very strong emotions I was experiencing. And I didn't understand the cause of these feelings, and why they were so strong as to bring tears. What had happened, was a I had heard one particular stick game song for the first time. It occured to me, this is such a beautiful song, and I was overcome with emotion. Part of our losses is our ability to respond to beauty and mystery the way our ancestors probably did. We have lost our ability to enjoy and appreciate the beauty that is part of the remnants to which we hold and cling.

The losses of the ceremonies is presented as a romantic tragedy by mass media. They completely misunderstand the consequences of ceremonies. The ceremonies were the ways we communicated with the real powers in life. Prayers are fundamental to all human activity. With the loss of ceremonies we lost our prayers. With the loss of prayers, we lost our way of healing. Our strength as a people diminished as our ability to pray diminished.

Losses always deal with pain and suffering. The separation from a loved one can lead to depression if a person is not wholesome enough to handle it. Pain and suffering require recovery and healing before a person can get back to living. We never dealt with the pain and suffering over the loss of ourselves. The healing process in dealing with pain and suffering from a loss is called grieving. That was part of the problem of not knowing what we lost. So we're never quite "all there", because a part of us is missing, "lost!"

William James in his wonderful book, "the Varieties of Religious Experience", states that the path to healing starts with the realization that there is this something missing in ourselves. We come to realize that we aren't alright, and that somehow the path to healing is a spiritual path. He even states that many of us start this process even before we are aware that we are doing it.

Grieving and periods of mourning are critical to all cultures. There is a specific start, and an end to the period. I know there are various individuals examining ways on how a whole people can mourn the loss of themselves. This is vital to many of those camped in that hard place. One wonders, how did they find their way to searching for answers in this way. How did they arrive at the decision to find ways of mourning?

There is in the teachings from Christ, a very comforting promise expressed in one the Beatitudes, "blessed are they that mourn, for they shall be comforted". Maybe we have missed something pretty obvious, the sequence calls for mourning before we receive comfort.

Lets develop some meaningful grieving ceremonies, involve the whole community. Tell them honestly that we are grieving the loss of ourselves, due to the onslaught of the dominant culture.

It is the start of healing and wholesomeness. Once grieving is complete we can get on with living. We can start that living with a revitalization or revival of Indian spirituality. We can get on with that journey to discover ourselves.

There are many paths to recovery, healing, and fulfillment. It should be clear by now that we believe the ways are all spiritual. It requires a journey inward to meet that which we hid away from the world, and ourselves. As was already mentioned it is a meeting with ourselves, our true selves, in the vision quest. Lets avail ourselves of the opportunity to say "I've been to the mountain top".

Where we find our true selves is also where we find our Creator. It is here where you'll find two of the best friends you'll ever have or need, your Self and your Creator! Perhaps they are one and the same.

A new tradition is a catchy phrase. People indentify old Indian culture as traditional. And now all of this effort in self examination we're putting forth must lead us somewhere. There is a purpose we have in mind, where the rewards have to be substantial, otherwise why bother?

We are products of American Culture and American Tradition, whether we think so or not. "Monday Night Football", "the Pepsi Generation", "Its Miller Time", "Rock n Roll!", the personal computer, the job, the four wheel drive, Christianity, the scientific method, and money, all of these are thoroughly ingrained in each of our individual psychological composites. To remove that from our personality, to become less and less of ourselves, just isn't possible.

The thousands or hundreds of years our ancestors lived here, it is a good probability that customs changed. Patterns of behavior and thinking, changed and adapted, otherwise these tribes would have died out or would have been wiped out by competition. We've always adapted as a strategy of survival. Now is the time to adapt again.

The White Man's Bull is our Enemy

"There was this Wenatchee man who lived here about the time the Su-Ya-Pi started coming into this area. His name was T'Na-Wa-Kwut, he was the great great-uncle of Cecelia Ann Dick. He was an Indian Doctor with some rather developed capability. The incident we will talk about happened in an area called the Kolockum, South of present day Wenatchee.

Being active in providing for his family, he hunted much to feed them. While hunting he came upon a strange creature, one he'd never seen before. Seeing the creature looked rather tame and unafraid, T'Na-Wa-Kwut walked up to it. He was a knowledgeable and inquisitive individual, and something new to the environment aroused his curiosity. As he got close to the creature, he saw horns, and the creature still appeared calm and unalarmed. But when he got right up to the creature it hooked him and gored him in the belly. We who familiar, are very careful about walking up to a bull. But he didn't know, and so the bull gored him, and it ripped open his belly and his entrails spilled out. He kept his guts in his stomach with his hands, as he made the trip back to camp.

Normal medicine would have made death the prognosis for this type of injury. The people in his camp were very sure he was going to die, some even began to mourn him. He told his womenfolk to get some cleaning rags and hot water to wash his entrails and stuff them back into his stomach cavity. They did this and bound up his belly with buckskin.

He told his people, "I'm going into my camp for three days, and I don't want you to disturb me in that time, no matter what you may hear." So he went into his camp for three days of solitude to sing and pray for healing. The people could hear him sing for awhile, then there would be a period of silence, the silence would increase their uneasiness, but then he would start singing again. This continued for three days, just as he said he was going to do for the ceremony. It was during the periods of silence that the women would get concerned and want to check in on him, but the menfolks reminded them of their instructions. They put water under the flap of his camp, and since it disappeared, they assumed he was taking water.

When three days were up, he came out and showed his belly to the people. There was no sign of his injury, and his stomach appeared in good condition.

The song he sang with conviction and much faith to bring about healing is the one we will sing. It is a song of power for healing. It is T'Na-Wa-Kwut's song, and it was given to us to help in healing."

This is from a Sweat Talk given a number of times by Mathew Dick Jr. It is important because it is metaphoric of what happened to Indian peoples as a whole, and where we are at in our spiritual development.

As a people, we are much like the person in this story. Something has ripped out our insides, something vital to our whole health and well-being. It is only now are we recognizing that we have been mortally wounded by something from the Whiteman. This woundedness is now part of our heritage. Recognition of this fact is critical and vital to our survival. When we recognize the injury, when we no longer deny the deep wound to our spirit, we can commence the healing process.

It is a given that Indians are going to confront racism in all its manifestations in the American society. The challenge to our people is find a process to minimize or neutralize the conditioning and indoctrination of inferiority. Then we must find a means to maintain and enhance our own humanity, and in our own minds, that of the non-Indian. We must find a means to live within this framework, which allows us to give to ourselves and those we share this world with, the utmost respect and dignity.

Stories like the one just presented are metaphors for our spiritual development. For a period of time we have went through life convinced that we were less than the non-Indian. The underlying theme of much of what Indians must go through for healing the mind, body, and soul, is to change the precept that we are inferior to non-Indians. We must find a process to cleanse and purify ourselves from this dangerous frame of mind.

As was already mentioned this indoctrination comes from the education, religious, and political institutions of non-Indian society. There are prerequisites to solving the problem: first - bring awareness of what has occurred; second - come up with countermeasures for prevention and or the practical means of healing; third - communicate the problems and the solutions. We will carry on healing unique to the Indian heart and soul. So we look to the elements of making people wholesome and healthy that have been available to us already for a millennia.

The activities we envision are integral to living. The changes are of a second order change. This means not only changing the behaviors and habits that are proving fatal to us, but we have to insitute wholesale change in values and beliefs. This is no small feat by any measure. The changes have to be intrinsic, something basic and fundamental to our character and nature is to be transformed.

Like T'Na-Wa-Kwut, our internal vitals have been ripped out and exposed, and now they have to be washed and put back in order. T'Na-Wa-Kwut's healing process involved his personal "Medicine" or "Power". In the reality of his world, there was no segregation of mind, body, and spirit. If there was injury or illness in the body, there was subsequent dis-ease in the mind and spirit, and vice-verse. The healing process was ritualized and ceremonial, because it took the whole person into consideration.

The healing we are missing is the healing of our spirit. In the healing of the spirit or soul, we look at the spiritual activities. These will be ritualized, and ceremonial, involving beauty and mystery, because of the symbolic nature of the way the our spiritual nature perceives and comprehends..

The scientific method or thinking has to be brought into alignment with this frame of mind. Much of the beauty of the beliefs held by our ancestors has been diminished in our own minds, because we have been educated. Our minds have been conditioned to think along the lines of the scientific method. This mindset tells us that the creation we inhabit, follows physicals laws only, that there is nothing to prove that the spirit exists, in all of this. The rationality of our programmed logic, prohibits or inhibits much of what our spirituality tells us is possible. The thinking limits the possibilities, this implies that our thinking determines what we experience as reality. T'Na Wa Kwut's thinking didn't have the limitations that we have imposed on ourselves.

Because it isn't objective much of what we are considering is denied by scientific or rational thinking. We will be in the frame of mind that originates in our intuitive nature. There is nothing rational about basing our actions and decisions on a feeling or a hunch, but somehow these are our best decisions.

For many years after the incident with the bull, the camas diggers from among the Wenatchee were warned, "The bull is your enemy". The bull represents much of the new but unseen threats to the integrity of our being, that come with being part of non-Indian society.

"...This Indian chief had a son who had died rather young. The death of this son left a young widow, who still grieved her loss. This Chief also had another son who was nothing like the son that died. The son that died was well respected among the people. The son who still lived was generally regarded as "A Good for Nothing." He was referred to as I-yi-yush. He was dirty and filthy from not paying attention to his personal hygiene. As a result his body was covered with sores. As was a custom in those days the brother usually took his sister-in-law as a wife if his brother happened to die.

This one young man got up and went to her, he sneaked into her teepee at night, and offered to be her husband. She was appalled and insulted. She thought how could he think she could marry someone like him. He was dirty, he had sores all over his body. The sores were scabby and draining pus. She refused to marry him.

He went away for a while, to be by himself in the mountains, for a period of a summer and fall. In this time he was getting "Shumachk", he talked to many of the animal spirits. In the fall he came around the south end of Lake Wenatchee and found a place he felt was good for a sweat house. During this time he sweated five days and nights all by himself. When he came out he was purified, he was sure of it.

He built a raft and went out to the center or middle of Lake Wenatchee. He rolled off the raft, into the deep water, and went to the bottom of the lake. He landed next to a teepee that was made for a very powerful person. From inside he could hear a meeting going on, and he could hear various conversations. The leader stopped everyone and said, " I hear something fall outside next to our camp. I want someone to go out and look to see what it is". Bear and Loon went out and saw this young man laying there next to their teepee. They went back in the teepee and told this chief or leader, "It's a human person laying out there. But we can see something dirty in his stomach, you probably won't want to talk to him or see him". The chief replied, "Well, okay, if he has something dirty about him, send him out". Bear and Loon went outside the teepee, they grabbed the young man and threw him out of the lake. The young man landed on the shore of the lake next to his sweat house.

He thought to himself, " Well I know I sweated long and hard to purify and cleanse myself, but I guess there is something left in me that is unclean". For five more days and five more nights, he sweated. He again got back on his raft and went to the center of the lake, he rolled of his raft, into the deep water, to sink to the bottom of the lake. Again he landed next to this teepee of this important person. The chief heard him land and told Bear and Loon to investigate once more. Bear and Loon went out and saw the young man again. They went back to the chief and said, "It's that same human person, but that dirty thing in his stomach is gone, maybe you will want to talk with him this time." The chief said, "Well, alright, he has tried real hard, so we should hear what he has to say. Bring him in."

When the young man came before the chief, he saw that the chief was a great and very impressive elk. This elk told the young man, "I know you've been talking with all the animals, I know you've been getting lots of Shumachk. Since you worked so hard to talk to me, I am the last one you will have to talk to. And because you made such a serious effort, I will help you. When I help you, that is all the help you will need." He told the young man to return to his parents and put on a dance for three days and he would help him and his people.

When he returned to his parents and people, it caused quite a stir. When the widow saw him all his sores were gone, and so were the scabs and pus. He was changed and she thought he was beautiful. She told him that she would marry him, but he no longer wanted to marry her. He had other things to attend to..."

From a Wenatchee Story by Cecilia Ann Dick, as told to her

71

children on Badger Mountain, during yealy trips to get camas.

This story and many more like it, have been a large part of the upbringing of area Indian children. It is amazing that they still teach important lessons in life. Many of the kids in our family would fall asleep and not hear the complete stories, so my grandmother would tell them repeatedly. The children knew them well enough to even request a certain story. Besides being teaching about life, the stories were very entertaining. These stories are the connections or vital links to the generations that preceded us. Within them lie the formulas for healing and health.

There is poetry in this oratory. The story teller interwove her own life into the fabric of the story, so she was as important to the message as the story was. The storyteller had the heart and soul of the people and could communicate the process of living. It is how the lessons continue today. We have spent much time listening to the living link with our past.

I can understand the young man wanting the woman to marry, she represented something from his deepest basic desires, and something very unattainable. Today we crave the certain things simply because everybody else craves that particular thing. We want the things that give us status and prestige. And whether we want to admit it or not we want the approval of the non-Indians. This approval comes by denying who we are in reality, and submitting to the indoctrination of inferiority. Because this desire is not founded in our hearts and souls but from our desires, it is unattainable.

Like the young woman who thinks the young man has the nerve, that "dirty bugger", we crave something that is unattainable. It is good that this is the case, it will not make us a healthy and wholesome people. Like his loathsome qualities, this wanting of approval from an external source, is loathsome. We should be able to provide it ourselves. It is only fitting and right that this approval should be withheld.

We need to go away by ourselves and purify ourselves. We must cleanse ourselves of our petty and trivial wants. We must become free of our fears. When we come back from our isolation we should be purified. We should become beautiful.

And we should be too good for the woman who spurned us, who now wants us. We should be purified, and rise above being a people driven by petty wantonness and cravings. We must become motivated by our higher needs. The assistant chief of police has already so eloquently stated, "We need to learn how to be good human beings."

Purifying ourselves is the key. For thousands of years there have been practices for such purposes. The peoples indigenous to this region kept themselves healthy. The practices were holistic. The practices were integrated with the other pursuits in the making of a living. So we go back to that which was unique to ourselves, to help ourselves, to purify ourselves.

Lake Wenatchee represents our individual spirits. We have to work real hard to get to the middle or center of ourselves. We must get to the bottom of ourselves and talk to the Chief, who is our higher self, our true self. We must be very honest, sincere and earnest in this effort, this way the Chief will help us and our people. The above story was one of the earliest I can remember.

Preparation and committment to achieving purification and cleansing, require discipline. We have already stated that we have lost much from what our ancestors practiced as a discipline for health. Would we be able to sweat for ten days? Do we have the ability to go out by ourselves to talk to the spirits? Do we have the stability in our mental faculties to withstand an encounter with the sacred? The Chief in the story is generous and understanding. If we use all of our capabilities, what little there is left, that should be sufficient. The Chief says "I'm the last one you will have to talk to". For people in search of meaning and direction in life, this is very significant. We have a way to get to our real selves. Like at the bottom of Lake Wenatchee, there camps a very important person, within ourselves. Lake Wenatchee is like our spirits, we have been moving all around the water along the surface, along the peripherory, it is time we go within.

Now we come to discussion around and about the Sweat. In no way do we refer to it directly, like we have specific knowledge, we all can share. It is like trying to talk about wisdom, we can talk about the effects and results of wisdom.

But what is it? We know the results of properly participating regularly in a sweat. But why are the results so profound and rather spectacular?

In my conscious thought was the idea that the sweathouse and associated practices of purification were the way of our people. The knowledge was stored in a museum in my mind. It was something interesting and made for good remembrances in conversations among relatives. I never understood it in its practicality. I didn't possess the awareness that these same practices could be applied in my life to make me a better human being.

In long buried memories, the sweathouse was a torture chamber, and a test of endurance for me as a youngster. I considered the practice to be, a matter of hygiene. I was only half right. It was a matter of hygiene, although more than providing a clean body like I had supposed. The practices were also intended to clear the spirit, help a person get rid of a bad heart.

A person giving a talk while partaking in a sweathouse ceremony got me reacquainted with what it actually is. It is certainly nothing from a museum. It is as contemporary as the work I do on a computer. I was told that all Indians consider the sweatlodge as something with sanctity. My grandmother says "it is the Womb of the Mother Earth. We go into it to become reunited with the Mother. While we are reunited, we are cleansed and purified. When we come out, we are renewed, we are reborn."

"Wi' Ta-T'u-Pia!"

"Wi' Ta-T'u-Pia!" means "Hello Great-Grandmother !", spoken with a prayerful attitude. In some cases the focus is on "Grandfather", but it is highly important to understand that the address might even be more intimate. A child says "Grandpa! or Grandma!" This is the type of relationship implied in the prayer. We address the great difference in wisdom and understanding, in our prayer.

There was a startling change in my relationship to the Earth, when I first heard this, and started using the prayer myself. There was an awakening or a reawakening of my spirit. In our inner awareness, we have come back to the Womb for purification, cleansing, and renewal. The Earth always reminds us that the process of life is birth, death and renewal. We have come back to the sweathouse for renewal. Something inside many of us has died, we need to rebirth it.

I went to a sweat for the first time after some forty years. While I was in there, it was the same torture chamber. But I wasn't going to be the first one to bail out. When I was young I would sometimes have to say, "Grandpa! I can't breath, I have to get out!" And of course I would jump out before I was complete. This time I sat there and prayed. I endured the heat, the discomfort, and pushed right on through the need to get out. Before I knew it, I was quiet, my own thoughts didn't even intrude. Without effort and striving intentionally, it just happened. The best description I can make, is I found myself in the "Presence". And much of what I needed to communicate was accomplished without words, so to speak. This Presence was very tolerant and made me feel like an absent-minded relative, who just happened to forget to come and visit often enough. To say the least I was comforted and purified.

For many who try to pray in the sweathouse for the first time, experience the feeling they are being listened to, by kind receptiveness. That their worries and concerns are being taken as valid. Some have experienced positive or affirmative responses to their prayers. The people who do sweat, experience a sense of well being, peace of mind, and serenity.

It has been claimed from practitioners that the sweat is a place to gather wisdom. This is a rather unusual use of the term. But development of the intuitional senses seems to have happened. Participants indicate that they are more generous, compassionate, and more effectively helpful to people. They report some of the answers to problems, come not from their individual experience, but from somewhere deep within themselves.

It is important to point out that the adherents are very committed to a regular discipline of using the sweat as a consistent manner of praying. The practice continues even in the coldest of winter days, may decline in the hot summer days. The desire to become a better person through spiritual exercise seems to be all that it takes to start. There is graphic evidence of growth both emotionally and spiritually in those that have partaken. There is competence expressed in the ability to meet everyday challenges. There is great faith expressed in th meaning of all events one experiences, that what we go through is meaningful and significant. Sometime during the practice of the sweat, we have reacquired the purpose and direction of our lives.

We go on that spiritual journey we propose inducing into our people. We go to meet our true selves, and rid ourselves of the fear, hatred, and resentment, if you're like me, we harbor towards the non-Indian. We forgive, accept, and tolerate in a fashion we ourselves deserve. We do so, because it would be beneath our dignity to do otherwise. This is also purification, part and parcel of becoming a good human being.

Getting Our Focus

A new tradition, although catchy isn't what will happen from our efforts. What will happen is a continuation of the integration and a synthesis of our contemporary experience and that which survived from our aboriginal culture. We explore new ways and meanings by which we will bring our true selves to meet the world. It looks so simple and easy, but many have died already rather than try it.

We will go find our true selves, maybe the way George and Melvin do it. If we are going to show or teach somebody something, it has to be a part of our internalized experience. We have to be examples, we have to "walk our talk!"

What we find will be universal human activity, that will become part of our values and beliefs, when we pass it on to posterity, we'll have a tradition. If what we find strengthens and revitalizes our people, if it helps us to love and accept ourselves as we are, then we have something that might become a new tradition. Right now all we're doing is finding a new trail, - we're explorers, - we're trailblazers!

How is a new pattern or model of living developed that will be the foundation to transformation and reformation? Again since we're in the exploration stages of our -effort, we'll examine, test, and experiment. That which humanizes, that which will provide an alternative to ego gratification, will be used repeatedly. Repetition of useful activities that help us grow, will in time become habitual, or programmed, or internalized. A number of people have already stated that prayer is the one common factor in a number of our individual transformations. Because we're trying to recover what we've lost, it will be praying in a uniquely Indian manner. So we're probably going to involve singing, dancing, sweat-house activity, reviving our ceremonies, reviving our spiritual exercises, possibly sharing experience and testimonials, and of course, the

Vision Quest. Much of the sharing of wisdom and experience occurs now in what is called the Talking Circle.

Many people looking for guidance in this area have doubts. How will we know it will be right for us? We've already mentioned that if the activity brings us closer to each other, or if it helps us grow in tolerance, love, and compassion, it is probably right. If the activity is conducive to healing and wholesomeness, it is probably good for us. When one involves spiritual activity, intuition will tell much about what is good and useful.

The new model or pattern for the recovery of dignity seems to be a person dedicated to reliance on a spiritual guidance. A morning prayer and meditation will start this person's day. A gathering and sharing with a fellowship of common adherents, on maybe a weekly basis. This experience already happening among some of our people, is the powerful effect of the Talking Circle.

The gathering could be facilitated by the Sweat, which is the natural place for the preparation of the individual to commit to the Vision Quest. The person will continue practicing the procedures of conducting a Vision Quest in retreats, and finally undertake a Vision Quest. To maintain any progress or growth would require sharing of strength, experience, and hope with new participants. Such has been the example of the Twelve Step Recovery Programs and the Cursillo with its Altreya. In communion with the larger community to affirm and acknowledge growth and spiritual progress, with dances and similar gatherings, the individual achieves belonging.

Will there be a consensus of what is right for us? Not likely! We're a fractious and quarrelsome bunch of people. Jealousy must be guarded against even in a small group like the one here. Even in the first meeting it seemed everyone was kind, polite and considerate, there were people who felt slighted and insulted. The best thing I know, is to pray for guidance when trying to arrive at a decision.

It should be remembered that what ever we come up with will be a synthesis of many ideas, concepts, disciplines, practices, and solutions. The source of which will be many cultures, religions, philosophies, and traditions. Our one common agreement is to revive the cultural aspects of Indian-ness, that was lost.

The product of a synthesis is a synthetic. This used to be a detrimental term. That was when what we refer to as a synthesis was new in practice in industry, such as chemical processes. But synthesis has always been occurring. Photo-synthesis is the process of plants converting light to sustenance by synthesizing it with minerals and water. Our bodies synthesize food into fat, bone, muscle and various other bodily tissues. Our minds synthesize various data from our senses into conclusions about reality. Again these various conclusions are synthesized into thoughts, thoughts into ideas, ideas into beliefs and concepts, etc.

Synthesis is a scientific term. What our people and society in general will find most empowering will be the synthesis of science and spirituality. Our spiritual nature needs the magical, and the fantastical. Science can't explain such phenomena, so it has to deny the existence of such. The spiritual nature needs to conduct much of its reality in faith, science seems to be the antithesis of faith. The spiritual nature needs emotion and feeling, science avoids it like the plague under the guise of objectivity.

But as science progresses into things like astro-physics, quantum physics, they are leading the way towards accepting something like subjective reality in the scientific methodology. Examination of the so-called para-normal is being studied. A new field called para-psychology has evolved where more lee-way is given to explaining phenomena previously denied by science.

This is particularly important to Indians because science needs to share in the sacredness we have towards the earth. Our time here is relatively short, but in that short time we've all managed to literally shit in our nest. A big part of recovering dignity is a return to the honoring of and holding reverence for our world.

"I've been blessed because I'm here In this awesome and beautiful world" Reverence is what signifies our uniqueness as a species. It is what keys our spiritual growth and progress. We don't worship nature but revere it because it is an extension and manifestation of the creative process of the Maker.

The Sharing of Wisdom - of Caring

There is something divine or sacred in doing a Twelve Step call. This is the process in the Twelve Step Fellowship where members go and carry a message of recovery to a suffering individual they think is ready to hear the message. This is the whole program, this is what insures the person a successful participation in life as well as the Fellowship. Early on when I was just starting, I went on these calls with very few successes. The miracle of the program is that they did me more good than the persons I was trying to help. Whether it is your intention or not, you become the instrument of that "Higher Power". Each time I tried, it affirmed that I was doing the right thing, and that with a little more knowledge and practice I would get successful.

There is nothing more challenging in life for a person, than to execute a shift in entire personal systems of emotional values and beliefs, or developing a new ethic. It is a terrific struggle for the person trying to do so, made easier by these efforts to carry the message. It is the first time many people in this position are going to discover they are empathetic or compassionate. It is the first time many of them will demonstrate their reverence toward a god of some sort. It is these actions on a consistently regular basis that creates the change in a person.

The person going through these contortions of the spirit, early on, doesn't think that is what is going on though. That person is told "Hang in there, it will get better!", do it "One day at a time", or "Easy does it, but do it!" Quillen Chuten in one translations means "the Worker of Man", it is highly appropriate in these kinds of situations. People become more of themselves in spite of themselves, helping others even when their intentions are selfish, as it was in my case, in trying to Twelve Step someone else.

Every one involved has come through a common experience. Everyone understands the desolation, the humiliation, the

81

degradation, the pointless and useless existence of being a drunk. Somehow, sharing this experience honestly, helps the people transcend themselves. The result is a "Spiritual Awakening", being helpful and useful to people will start the process.

The Cursillo is just as potent in bringing about this type of change in a person. The Cursillo is an "encounter" in every sense of the word. The people involved, share their experience of living apart from their God. After the encounter there is a rebirth of the spirit in the person. The changes are as drastic and for the better, as those experienced by the Twelve Step Fellowship. The encounter is one of personal participation in beauty, mystery, and ceremony, that involves the total person.

The candidates as well as the team putting on the Cursillo sing, pray, dance, create dramas, create humor, create stories, work together as a team, and share intimately common experiences in life. During this process the candidates undergo a profound change. Many claim this is a transformation of the spirit, others claim it is a rebirth, or being born again. In any case it is brought about by bringing the candidate into an active, participating relationship with God.

In the end there is a sharing among the candidates. I witnessed one after the other, men, who were what I thought were lost causes, real hard cases, break down and cry with happiness. I thought I was immune to this. On the way home the first Cursillo I attended, I remembered one individual whom I thought would and could resist the encounter. He stated "You all know me, ...we've fought each other, ...we've stole each other's women, ...been really bad towards each other. I just don't know what's happened, ...but I'm so happy for you!" He then commenced to crying uncontrollably. I was driving home, about thirty miles from where the Cursillo was held, when I remembered this, and I started crying uncontrollably.

The effects of both of these groups is startling. An observer is always amazed at the transformations. In each case they are drastic, totally out of character of the candidates, and can be termed miraculous. If a person quits associating with either of these groups, the effects diminish or disappear altogether, and the people resort to form.

At the heart of the questions brought up by some of the people who experienced the failure to change was, "Why do I have to become a white-person, why not be an Indian?" We need a process where people can be themselves to be able to affect change in themselves on a permanent basis. At that deepest part of the self, when one meets God, one should be able to present the real self. The real self should be good enough in all cases.

A process we could contemplate would be one of initiating a relationship with a spiritual being. Basically all that is needed to start, is a willingness. The process could be carried out in prayer and ceremony. The ceremony would be one based on mystery, and on beauty with songs and dances, with regularity. The effort to propagate such a process would be carried out by the membership carrying the message of the group. Part of the ceremony would be sharing of the common experience of living. Because as we grow we realize we are sharing that most precious gift from the the Creator, we share part of our life. We share with those we want to help most. The content of teaching and sharing would be acquired by self discovery.

The progress of a person's life, being proposed here, would be to: become aware of the situation or condition that makes us unhealthy or unwholesome; learning new practices of praying and meditating to heal ourselves; learning to conduct spiritual ceremonies of healing to help others; regular times for commitment to a search; and then conducting self discovery; and finally relating and sharing these self discoveries.

It would be totally Indian in nature, coming from the various Indian cultures we have available to draw on. It wouldn't be exclusive in nature at all. There would be no rejection of some type of cultural practice or ceremony because it came from "those Nez Perces, or those Plains Indians". From this we can expect "Vision Quests, Dances, Dinners, Giveaways, Namings, Sweats, and whatever else a group finds acceptable on a consensual basis.

The process in and of itself wouldn't be one of conversion to a new religion or spiritual practice. Its main purpose should be to interrupt the way a person thinks and feels currently about life.

And as the person grows, direct them to the Twelve Step Fellowship, the Cursillo's Fourth Day, the Seven Drum, the Shakers, or any other endeavor which is spiritually purposeful. It should be planned for a person to utilize the process for spiritual growth. As with most spiritual activity, the growth and progress are endless and the possibilities are infinite.

The Talking Circle

None of the activities we contemplate undertaking are done in solitude nor in isolation. With the possible exception of the Vision Quest, all activity we are talking about are undertaken in a community of sharing and fellowship. Again is the presence of the sharing of wisdom and experience, again we find a focal point in the Talking Circle.

When a group or a community gathers to meet a challenge, an exchange of ideas, of feelings, problems, solutions, and of aspirations, occurs. These are communications of the heart. The language spoken, is the language of the heart. In such groups there has to be a feeling of complete security about personal disclosures. Each person has to feel that their own individual contributions are valid and worthwhile to everyone else. And yet each person has to develope the courage to initiate the process for themselves.

Much of our community, families, and other close knit associations have members who have repressed the ability to express emotions. In the talking circle, there must be complete freedom and security in the expression of pain, fear, resentment, and sorrow. We need to practice this expression because it is a crucial part of what makes us human beings. This inability to express emotion properly is central to the need for healing of our people. It is part of our incompletness. Participation in the groups like the Talking Circle help in the healing and growth of individuals.

It is important that we move beyond our own bigotry. It is important that we develop the honesty and humility necessary to heal. Active involvement in the sessions for communication is vital. In the process of communion, we experience healing. Everything we learn and experience in the sweat, our dances, our ceremonies, and fasts will be shared as wisdom in the Talking Circle.

Part of the sickness of alcoholism is the loneliness and isolation people feel, even in the midst of a crowd of people. The circle is our entry back to community, and feeling acceptable as a person, starts here. Also in the case of alcoholics, are the instances of severely handicapped social skills. A child has complete safety and security to develop these in a family. A person on the road to healing needs such a place of security and freedom. A person on the road to healing needs much encouragement, support, and understanding.

The love, compassion, and understanding are the vital ingredients to bring people out of self imposed isolation. The Talking Circle, whether in a home, at work, or in the Sweat are the crucial to growth. It has been fashionable to talk about synergy. The circle will demonstrate quite vividly the synergy of such a group. Unity is empowering to people who have lost all personal power. When we stand together, bonded with our hearts and spirits, we are not afraid to solve the challenges that appear impossible to confront individually.

The circle of participants usually tracks the condition and progress of it members. Whether it is done intentionally or not there is some very powerful peer pressure exerted on members. In the most compassionate manner the members who might be conducting themselves in an unhealthy manner will be informed and enlightened. It is quite evident to the groups in activity now that the personal growth, whether spiritually or intellectually, builds on itself in this setting.

It is noteworthy that the sharing of wisdom is the main ingredient of the gatherings occurring now. The experience or personal discoveries are shared freely and willingly. The discoveries made generally deal with growth in personal awareness. Somehow the individuals incorporate these discoveries into their own personal wisdom.

These disclosures and sharing of personal experience come out in a highly emotional way. In this process we are witnessing the exorcism of personal demons of jealousy, hate, bigotry, guilt and fear. The effect is cathartic. We are always making the discovery that the healer is within us. That this healer is empowered by spiritual activity. In the groups of good hearts we

86

are able to call forth this healer who is at our individual centers.

It is highly necessary or almost a prerequisite to growth and healing to make this contact with others in similar situations to ourselves. It is so comforting to know we don't suffer alone, that our healing will proceed in a unity.

The Successful Example

The basis for a new pattern or model for living will be the process and practice of becoming the good human being. We have spent years waiting for someone else to confer on us validation and valuation that wasn't forthcoming. We kept waiting for someone else to recognize our inherent nobility, when we couldn't recognize it in ourselves. The good human being will recognize that dignity is intrinsic, it won't come from some external source. It will come only when we get to know our real selves. The evidence and examples for successful developments in this area can be found in the Twelve-Step Fellowship and the Cursillo Movement.

Each of these appears to be spiritual ministries without the central figures of preachers and prophets. Each is conducted in community or fellowship of more or less equals. Each teaches a total reliance on God and compassion for one's fellows. Each emphasizes that we help each other grow on the basis of humility. Each addresses our spiritual nature in its need for beauty and mystery through praying, meditating, singing, sharing, art, drama, and humor.

The Twelve-Step Fellowship and the Cursillo Movement have manuals or books to provide guidance that outline their principles. A similar document for our people is needed, something concrete for them to read and study and assimilate. In each case, the Big Book of the Fellowship and the Fourth Day of the Cursillo, outline practices that help people live better, to become better human beings.

Where else would we get principles defining honesty, humility, tolerance, acceptance, serenity, sharing and caring. Where else would we get a concept of the problem and recovery from racism. The Twelve Steps are an excellent model for recovery, and a program for living. I have taken the liberty of plagiarizing the steps into something of a model for the recovery of dignity.

It is noteworthy that like most people, I thought the Steps would severely restrict and restrain my freedom. Paradoxically I have enjoyed even more freedom, for now I have gained some freedom from self-centeredness, self-deceptions, self-pity, and general selfishness. I've awakened to all the possibilities God has lay at my disposal, my choice, to follow or not. The great redeeming quality of the Steps is the discipline they brought to my life. The steps have synthesized my spirituality from my people's culture and later Christian teachings.

The dominant feature of the Steps is that they are a program of spirituality. And it is from here I learned that the symptoms of soul sickness are more evident and obvious than the causes. One of the causes is our distancing ourselves from God, and living our lives in a shallow spiritual plane. In our distancing from God, we try to rely on ourselves. This self reliance becomes distorted and we become selfish, self-centered. When we encounter life's invariable challenges, and they only seem to overwhelm us, we become self-pitying. When our efforts to meet life's challenges come up short, we distort reality to conform to this distorted image, so instead of a dedication to reality, we are dedicated to an image, not based in reality. We become self-deceptive.

The steps are a program to teach humility and honesty. We need humility to rely on God, honesty to diagnose our inner problems. Like The vision Quest, the Steps lead you into a grand meeting with yourself and your Higher Power. They are brought up here because Indians confront the indoctrination of inferiority in the Twelve Step Fellowship. It isn't something overt, but it is certainly based in ignorance. There have been instances where Indians were told bluntly, "We aren't here to listen to you talk about the Creator, or the sweats, or various dances, we want to hear about *real* spirituality".

This is the case more often than the Fellowship likes to admit. Some Indians will try to conform to some perceived "standard spirituality", most however, when confronted with that attitude, leave. They may search for spiritual help elsewhere, or some other form of recovery, or they simply go back to drinking and die. Many stay are very helpful to other Indians trying to recover, still too many go back the alcohol or drugs. We want to give these people a place to begin the process of a spiritual awakening.

With all due respect and reverence I have adapted the Twelve Steps to a process of healing for people victimized by racism. It was a healthy excericise for myself, in dealing with the dark side of this victimization. I have also adapted the Twelve Traditions in a way that will help groups avoid the negative effects of "Jealousy, the bane of Indians", this helps with group and community survival.

"Twelve Steps to Recover Human Dignity"

1. We admitted we powerless and that our lives were unmanageable.

2. We came to believe that a Spiritual Being is our path to reality, in recognition that we suffered from the delusion we were inferior.

3. We made a conscious decision to turn our wills and our lives over to the care and guidance of this Spiritual Being.

4. We honestly, fearlessly, and with the best of our ability, examined ourselves in our attitudes, values, and beliefs, for the negative affects of being treated as a inferior people. Searching our inner-most selves for any prejudice and bigotry we may have harbored towards non-Indian people and institutions. We recorded our insights of our personal search.

5. We shared our insights with our Spiritual Guidance, and another human being, the exact nature of those insights.

6. We were ready and willing to shed ourselves of the

negative affects of being treated as a defeated people.

7. We humbly asked our Spiritual Guidance to remove these negative effects, especially asking to be freed from our own prejudices and bigotry towards non-Indian peoples and institutions.

8. We made a list of all the people and institutions we were prejudiced and bigoted against.

9. We made amends for our own prejudiced bigoted behavior, and asked to be reconciled with all human beings and our Spiritual Guidance for conduct beneath human dignity.

10. We were constantly vigilant in our own personal behavior for conduct beneath human dignity.

11. We continually practiced prayer and meditation to maintain our conscious contact with our Spiritual Guide, praying only for guidance and the power to follow the guidance.

12. We would exemplify the good human being conducting ourselves with dignity and self-respect, and we seek to share our experience with others to show them how to do the same. We will be messengers of hope and instruments of our Spiritual Guidance.

As with many good intentions, what I've done here will probably be greatly misunderstood. But fools do rush in.

Self help is the key, if a person is genuinely trying to develop a manner of living that is dedicated to a reliance on a Spiritual Guidance. The entry into a fellowship or community is almost a prerequisite to successful self help program. Someone else must always be there to challenge our honesty and humility, someone else must always be there to challenge our ideas on spirituality. We also need others to remind us that we seek "spiritual progress rather than perfection" in the results from our efforts. There will be setbacks, and we will need each others support and encouragement.

The Twelve Traditions are a good frame work to help groups survive internal strife. As was already mentioned, we seem ready for a confrontation at the drop of hat. I've never seen anything better at facilitating consensus than the Twelve Traditions. Again I've taken liberties with changing the wording of the originals but hopefully not the essence.

Our Principles of Community Survival

1. Our common welfare and improvement should come first, personal healing and recovery of our dignity and self-respect depends on our reliance on our Spiritual Guidance and on each other.

2. There is but one ultimate authority, the Spiritual Guide, that is expressed through a group conscience, our leaders are but trusted servants, they do not govern.

3. The only requirement for membership and participation is the desire to become a better human being by overcoming the indoctrination of inferiority.

4. Our common heritage is what brings us together, we will stay together only by our personal choice.

5. Our primary purpose, as an affiliation of like minded persons, is to carry the message on the recovery of dignity. We strive to be instruments of hope and examples of spiritual growth and improvement.

6. We must never allow problems of money, property, or prestige, divert us from our primary purpose. We strive to be apolitical in our views and activities relative to the group.

7.   We are self-supporting through own financial resources.

8.   We will consider everyone a non-professional in matters of Indian spirituality.   Everyone's opinion and contributions will be treated equally.

9.   We will not be organized, but we may create committees, or work groups directly responsible to those they serve.

10.   We will express no opinions on outside issues, that way we will never be drawn into public controversy

11.   Our public relations policy is based on attraction rather than promotion.   We need always maintain personal anonymity at the level of press, radio, films, and television.

12.   As human beings we will rely heavily on spiritual principles, and it is to principles rather than individual personalities, we acknowledge as our source of healing and recovery.

It is with a firm belief and strong expectation that if a process for healing is undertaken on the reservation, people to people will be the channel by which it is executed. The Spiritual Guidance will come through people trying to help people. The messages of hope and strength will come through people. The "Word of God" will come through poeple. These people will need to associate with each other if they have a common purpose.   Most self help fellowships have a slogan that says, "We can do what I couldn't do by myself".

Groups, fellowships, or communities will develop, and at the heart of these communions is the sharing of ourselves.   The survival tactics a person utilized to stay alive, are generally the same tactics that keep a person separated from God and one's fellows.   This is greatly changed by the process of sharing in a gathering, the sharing is usually in a semi-formal setting.

In the sharing one discloses personal experience regarding the stages a person goes through in the search for dignity. The progression through these stages is marked by the steps. As with the steps of the Twelve Step Fellowship, if we work our steps with the most honesty and to the best of our ability, personal and spiritual growth is achieved. These are just a recommendation because, as was previously mentioned, we are seeking to direct someone to more thorough spiritual practices.

But for people who decide to work the previously outlined steps, they need to be worked in all honesty, with a full commitment to succeed. The steps are meant to help a person acquire honesty, humility, and courage to carry out the practices of the Sweat, involvement in a community or fellowship of sharing, commitment to the vision quest, and finally undertaking the vision quest itself.

The steps are a tool or a method to establish and maintain a relationship with a Spiritual Guidance. This relationship is of a spiritual nature. This whole process is called a spiritual awakening. The changes are drastic and the person is profoundly changed. The process is intended to guide a person intact spiritually and psychologically to its conclusion. This type of spiritual awakening is of the educational variety.

At some point in time after serious and honest effort, a person recognizes in themselves, the realization of spiritual principles. Where before we were constantly fooling ourselves, we have developed a sense of responsibility to be honest to ourselves. We have become humble, become teachable, and know we are no more or no less than others in this world. We will learn to love ourselves, then we will learn to love others. At some point in time after our most serious, honest and diligent efforts, that old "inferior" person will become a thing of the past. We will acquire dignity, we will see ourselves as God sees us.

As a person progresses through the Sweat Ceremony, involvement in a fellowship of sharing, commitment to the vision quest, and finally the vision quest itself, the steps serve as a framework for sharing and growth.

The Little Course & Talk

The Cursillo has had a great impact on the Indian community. Approximately one thousand people have participated in at least one on this reservation alone. There always seems to be a drastic personal change for the better among the participants. The follow up process, the Altreya, is what amounts to a maintenance process for this change and transformation. The most striking aspect of the Cursillo is the tremendous emotional and intellectual exhilaration experienced by the participants, some categorize this as spiritual high.

The most vital aspect of the Cursillo is the involvement of the members of the community to minister to the candidates. This is central to the success, since the community ministers have experienced the same challenges to living as the candidates. In this ministry, is the talk based on the life of the speaker, a sharing of personal experience. The candidates see the strength and hope they crave, in the message from the "Rollisto" or "Rollista", the presenter of the talk of or the "Rollo".

I have included an example of a talk on the lay ministry. This too, is highly appropriate to our effort. Having participated in Cursillo's, I have developed a high regard for the positive impact it has on the participants. The problem is getting candidates to the event. The privilege was actually mine in giving a Rollo at a Cursillo in February of 1993. In this process I think the presenter benefits more then the recipients of this "talk" or Rollo. It is included here because, as I said I benefited more than those who had to sit and listen to it. I also want to use it as an example for sharing in any process our group may eventually develop.

"Cursillo February 1993, Laity Rollo
I would like to express my humblest gratitude to the team for allowing me to share this talk with you. I was being

a couch potato at my mom's house when I volunteered.

I approach this talk with some excitement because I'm presented with an opportunity to make a positive contribution to someone's life. I will make an earnest and honest attempt to speak from the heart. As we progress I hope we'll transcend to speaking in the language of the heart. It is my fervent hope that at least one of you will find something in this talk, that is useful in the adventure of your life.

I have to restrain myself, and pray for humility, I need to ask God to help me stay out of the way of the message. I know the team will pray that I am able to conduct myself with honesty and insight.

Everything I say here has been garnered from someone else, either from books, meetings, conversations, and personal meditations. These ideas represent nothing original, but once I put my "profound" understanding, and "eloquent" interpretation to them, they become mine. They are therefore private, personal, and precious,-- and I wish to share them with you.

Everything I say will in one way or the other deal with one of the central values of my life, the dignity of man.

The talk on Ideal calls on us to be human beings with Christ as the model of our being. If we look at the accomplishments and achievements of mankind, we see a contradiction of possibilities and potential. Through out our history we see evidence of this, we see the most holy or sacred, to the most foul and profane of manifestations, as man acts out his destiny. Man has been blessed with awesome and tremendous gifts that present us with infinite potential that is godlike. The problem is we haven't been given the automatic knowledge on how to use these abilities, sometimes it seems we're very fortunate to learn how to walk and chew bubble-gum at the same time. Some of you have heard that we've been given this tremendous gift without the owner's/operator manual.

To be human is a blessing, a very profound blessing, not a handicap as some would have you believe. So the call to be human, we can move toward this ideal in modelling our life on the life of Christ.

The Old Testament tells us when God was creating man He said, "We will make him in the image and likeness of Ourselves". We have this heritage to live up to. As we are able to more and more closely emulate the Ideal of Christ, we will reflect this Image and Likeness, we will manifest this Divinity in man. Grace is the divinity in man; the creative, harmonious, forgiving, compassionate, enlightening, and empowering, by its nature very compelling and assertive.

If we look at life of Christ we see that he was ultimately concerned about the quality of the lives of people. The lives of people are acted out in society. As the leader's manual states we need to act out the ideal of grace that doesn't happen in isolation. It is up to people like you and me to exemplify the ideal, to express our divinity, in such a manner to awaken people who haven't heard the news of the heritage of man.

If you're not of the clergy or of some religious order you're a layman, or part of the laity. This talk on laity will build on the ideal and grace talks.

The laity have a mission to call forth the ideal of humanity in the expression of their divinity. We are duty to bound show those who don't know their heritage, how to live with dignity by exemplifying the ideal.

The Model for our ideal was often moved by conditions or situations. Like us, somethings He encountered touched Him. The love and concern for people that caused Him to be moved is easier to understand as compassion. It is the basis of our work as Laity.

Things happen in our lives that we keep recalling for no apparent reason. One such incident happened to me in Vietnam, and I didn't understand its significance at the time.

So I want to tell you a Viet-Nam Story. I was there, - and I remember, - I wasn't drunk or stoned all the time. I was there for eight months starting in August of 1970. I was a radio technician, or radio repairman. I was stationed at Marble Mountain, a little outside Danang, which was a

Marine Corps chopper base, home of MAG-16.

As I previously mentioned I was drunk a lot, so much I got in trouble and subsequently transferred to Zulu Company. Being drunk a lot I wasn't aware of the other units in the group. When I heard Zulu, I should have had a clue of where I was going. This was an infantry company that provided perimeter security. This was during era of Vietnamization so there were a lot of people transferred there who'd been out in boonies, so being a REMF was a difficult transition for them.

When I arrived there, the whole company that wasn't on duty, was out in the street with all their belongings. Somebody had fragged the XO, and so we were in the middle of an investigation. We sat out in the street for three days.

This company was composed of mostly blacks, I mean the officers were white, the senior NCO's were white, there was a Mexican communications corporal, and me, the rest were black. For whatever reason, somebody had fragged the Executive Officer. They investigated the incident and prosecuted the guilty, and we got a new XO. Three weeks later they fragged the new XO. So we're sitting out in the street again. This time they changed CO's. We're still out in the street when the new CO arrives to meet us. Someone yells attention, and everybody gets up off the ground about as slovenly and casual manner as can be.

This new CO says he's from Arizona, he's mustang, always been infantry, been in country since 1966, hadn't been back to the states in ten years, been in the Corps for twenty-two years, a hard core lifer. He says he must be successful at shaping up problem outfits, cause that's what they keep giving him, and that's what will happen to us, we'll shape up. Like everybody else I conclude that there will be some rough times a head, nothing short a beating.

He says he doesn't do nothing special, but he makes up his mind, when he gets to a new company, that he'll make better fighting men out of them. A change started to come of the formation. I don't really recall the rest of what he said, but at the end of his address, every man was standing the way a fighting man should stand, when he being addressed by his commander.

He didn't see a company of trouble makers, he saw a company of fighting men, and said so. He appealed to the ideal of the Marine being a fighting man. His address was one of respect, because he lived and breathed the ideal he was calling forth. He was appealing to their higher needs, he showed them how they could conduct themselves with honor and dignity. This man's whole being was what the company aspired to be, he said I'll show you how to be what you want to be. A powerful example of leadership.

(After years of living in a drunken fog, many aspects of the events related to here, may have been distorted. First, like most alcoholics, I would rather lie than tell the truth, even when the truth was more exciting. It has been in my mind so long now that it has the ring of truth it.)

From the Vatican II Documents, on Laity, "...they are to hold in high esteem, professional skill, family and civic spirit, and virtues relating to social behavior namely honesty, justice, sincerity, kindness and courage..." These characteristics are valued by the laity. By their nature you can guess where these strengths are brought bear in the lay persons quest to exemplify Christ.

As Laity we are called to use our God given gifts to work with families, young people, isolated individuals, where we socialize, and where we work. We will use our talents in addressing problems causes and effects. The effects are the most obvious, here it is usually a matter of bringing immediate relief from some pain or suffering. Over the long term it means confronting the values or their lack of. Our main problem is that we keep addressing our main efforts to deal with symptoms of problems as manifested in obvious visual results. We never in our wildest dreams think of dealing with the causes of our problems at their source!

I believe it is vital to our community to address the family disintegration, the alienation of children from parents, family violence, violence out in public, various addictions to work, sex, gambling, and drugs. I say these are effects because the causes are the fundamental problems of our whole community. Although it is important to bring immediate comfort to victims of violence or abuse, it is even more important to get at the causes.

As I have said already the causes are the values or the lack of values that guide our behavior. What values are present when a young man chooses alcohol when confronted with boredom? Or why does a young man see no alternative to violence in solving family disputes? What causes parents to choose external activities over time with their children? What are the causes that compel parents gamble away the grocery money? Half of the reservation lives below the poverty line, the values that guide them to that way of life have to be confronted. Why is that the almost half of the better off tribal members are indifferent to the appalling condition of the other half, what values are represented here? Too many people have surrendered to learned helplessness, and dependance, they need a wake up call.

So as the team and candidates ponder some of these questions, the work of the Laity seems to be in engendering new values that are conducive to human dignity and self-worth. At least the long-term strategy for transformation would require this.

In our compassion for our brethren, we need to ask the important questions, and seek out the answers, and put the answers into action, in the spirit of tough love.

I come from a fellowship that has a joke that says " We're all here because we're not all there". This to me has very profound implications for people making a journey to God. All of us at some time in our life have felt that something intangible missing from ourselves. At a very crucial turning point in all our lives we felt we didn't fit, or we were incomplete, or we were consistently unfulfilled. We thirsted and hungered for something substantial but our needs weren't met. I had heard some people in the fellowship describe this as soul sickness.

Some of us have manifested the symptoms of this soul sickness in the form of: defeated or demoralized attitude towards life, feeling depressed, paranoid, unloved, full of self pity, inadequate, hateful or resentful, vengeful, misunderstood, confused, guilty, remorseful, a tremendous sense of humiliation and degradation. While experiencing these symptoms, we also manifested a total defiance against our condition and being grandiose, fantasizing about being somebody or something else where we were exalted to positions of great prestige or grand importance.

The solution to getting out of this type of predicament, in getting wholesome or complete, was in getting help from God through people. We had to overcome selfishness, self-centeredness, self-pity, and self-delusion, and replace these with honesty, humility, and compassion. It is an on going process, and it helps us keep the causes of the soul sickness at bay.

In the principles of the fellowship I belong to, there is one that states "We came to believe that a Power greater than ourselves could restore us to sanity". I was at this stage of my own personal growth where my sense of wholeness was beginning to return. The process of healing really began to be noticeable.

It was through the encouragement and support of compassionate people guided by spiritual principles that this could happen.

Many of us have gone to war, have chased after the woman who would become our wives, gotten into fights, pursued a career where we advanced towards the top positions, where we have tackled the important decisions of our lives that shaped us. That part of ourselves that helped make the decisions and choices, and many of them were life giving, were made through what we called the ego.

That part of us that insists on not being defeated. It may make adjustments, make compromises, and anything to adapt and survive, or hold together the integrity of our individual identity. It is part of our natural make up much like our body odor. When we're out in the mountains our body odor make the wildlife pretty much want to avoid us. Say we are in a social setting, our body odor will cause the "wildlife" to avoid us. This part of each and all us will have to be surrendered to a Higher Power.

In my journey to completeness, or wholeness, I come to recognize the need to participate in a relationship with something which I perceived that my very existence depended upon, this something has to be greater than me, and it is something I perceived as divine.

I became convinced It was always there, but that I made a conscious choice at some time in my life to ignore it.

Like many Indians on the Reservation, I went to St Mary's Mission. It was there that like most people around I was introduced to the Catholic Doctrine. Like everybody in that school, I was taught the Catholic catechism. I became an altar boy. In that period of my boyhood I developed a spirituality that I recall very nostalgically. I was possessed with a feeling of such sanctity and grace, such a closeness with God, a tremendous sense of well being or wellness. I knew it was the right way to be. It was the state of being that perhaps I craved later on in life, but it was missing.

I was just recalling the old Mass in which as an altar boy I was a participant. The beginning was a prayer-dialogue between priest and altar boy. It went with priest intoning, "Et intro ibo ad altare Dei". The acolyte, the altar boy, responded, "A Deim qui letificat juven tutem meum". -- "I will go to the altar of God, the God who is the joy of my youth".

I had lost this sense of well being because of the Catholic Church who were pretty much responsible for helping me find it in the first place. Somewhere along the course of this period I was told I would have to give up some pretty good things to stay close to God. Things like fun, flirting with girls, which seemed innocent enough, to some to the things I read. It's odd that I may have already been enculturated with right to make personal choices.

It seemed the hard choices required more courage than I could muster. The school planned to send me to Gonzaga Prep, and I new if I was sent there I was lost forever.

Also it seems coincidental that I began to recognize the

difference in treatment of Indians and non-Indians by the school. I began to recognize that the benevolence manifested by many in the church was the result of what I perceived as a sanctimonious and superior attitude. To this day I am infuriated by patronization and condescension. And regardless if this was the case or not, I decided to turn away from God.

Why turn from God?

When I was making these tremendous decisions in my life the Mission, the fathers, and nuns were to far away to turn away from, I was to chicken to confront them anyway.

The nuns at St. Mary's Mission were Dominican Nuns, what they called the Order of Preachers. Now preachers aren't going to preach to other people who know how to preach. The Dominican Order was established to practice their form of spirituality in the affairs of the world. It is pretty much the same with the Jesuits, the Soldiers of Christ, their order went on the offensive so to speak, like Force Recon, to carry out their missionary work.

When Christ decided to have dinner and associate with a bunch of tax collectors and women, the established religion of the day was affronted. They asked Him why do you associate with tax collectors and all these women. Christ's response was more like "the healthy don't need the Healer. I come to make whole the afflicted." It is here where most of us can fit into the model of Christ's life.

We aren't the Pope, the Curia or the Cardinals, none of us are Archbishops, Bishops, or Abbots, nor are we Priests, Brothers or Nuns. If you're a good guy, and you want to exemplify Christ in your life, and you're none of the aforementioned, or say you're not a professional at spreading the Gospel, then you're a lay person.

You're the foundation for the Church, without you there wouldn't be any need for the rest of those guys. The Church like all big institutions is always a little behind its constituents. The people who weren't the clergy or the religious wanted to be activists in exemplifying Christ. They didn't ask the Church, they just went out and did it. At times there is this big groundswell of lay people who respond to a compelling desire to do good for their fellow human beings. Like all good bureaucracies, the Church responded by taking charge of this groundswell and making sure that it was done according to it policies and procedures.

The term "lay" means "not of any profession". In today's world professional means you do it for the money, or some other mercenary reason. If you do something for the love of doing it, then you are an amateur. Professional also means being possessed of a high standard of excellence, a total commitment to the principles of the profession, that you are very disciplined to act on these principles. The clergy and the religious have felt a very compelling need to do what they do in what they refer to as the "The Calling". From what I gather it is irresistable. To be a professional in this area requires years of preparation.

The best lessons to learned about life are from life itself. The Church itself defined the lay person or collectively the Laity, as those who would act on their principles, values and beliefs where they lived. This is a very broad playing field. Where we lived was where we would find and help most of the unhealthy and the afflicted.

I mentioned I turned away from God. Finding God again and making this Divine Presence a part of my life was simple, but I made it rather difficult. I confused God with religion. I presumed that if you were to have a God you were to belong to a religion. The religion of my youth was full of contradictions that I couldn't resolve. But in spite of obstacles, raised mostly by myself, I found my way back to God.

As a part of the fellowship I belong to, I came to experience a very close and strong presence of God in my life. I've been greatly blessed. I got back my dignity and self respect. Fear of anything and everybody left me, and I felt capable to meet any challenge. I no longer felt like a failure, like I was inadequate or inferior. I knew that I had a purpose in life, and nothing that involved my life was trivial or insignificant. I experienced love, acceptance and understanding from other people. They treated me like I was somebody worthwhile, that what I had to contribute to life was worthwhile. They showed me to look for God in the last place I would have looked, which was within myself.

I came to believe in a Power Greater than Myself. I had to act on that belief to make it worthwhile. I made the decision to turn my will and my life over to that Higher Power. At the time I was only able to use the Fellowship and its principles as my Higher Power. The will of that Higher Power was to get better, quit settling for the things in life that were less than I deserved; to grow enough so I could take God as my Higher Power.

My life became turbo-charged so to speak. If you've seen the movie Scrooged, that was pretty much my reaction. I was reborn, rejuvenated, inspired to act, re-energized, or greatly empowered. Life became a great joy to participate in, and I began to participate. I got involved, at work, at play, within my family. I began to act on my beliefs and values where I lived.

In 1988 I made my Cursillo. If I was turbo-charged after my first spiritual awakening, the Cursillo lifted me into another dimension. It pretty much affirmed participation in life as good. I could look at the Catholic Church without some sense of hostility.

The last principle of the fellowship I'm in, states, "After having had a spiritual awakening, we tried to carry the message to those who still suffer...." I had greatly improved in praying and meditating. I made amends to people I had wronged. I told the people who helped me that they saved my life. They responded, "no it was the principles that saved you, and if you are truly grateful, you would pass on what you had learned and share what you had gained."

Early on in my time in the Fellowship, my father suffered a severe stroke. While everybody prayed he would live, I prayed to God he would die. My prayers weren't answered. After it became apparent that my father would live greatly impaired, I thought it time to face the music. In this time of struggle in dealing with this issue, a person similarly afflicted as me came into my life. My concentration and energy went to carrying the message of my recovery to this person. My concern for the way I prayed for my father was diminished.

One of my relatives died of Cirrhosis. I had tried to work with this individual, it seemed I couldn't do anything right. I remember our discussions ending up as one confrontation after another. In my prayers and meditations I told God I failed, and the answer was, "failed at what, you're charged with carrying the message. You think you had to save this person." While I was praying and looking for answers to this challenge another person came into my life to work with. And again my attention was focused elsewhere.

Lately I've become greatly concerned with my lot in life. I've become unemployed, and I feel I deserve better. While praying for guidance and assistance, some more people come into my life. And I am carrying the message of recovery in spite of myself. What keeps me from regressing to old patterns is this activity of carrying the message. It isn't an assertive or agressive activity, I don't go in pursuit of candidates. The afflicted are so pervasive, they find me wherever I am.

Well what does this have to do with anything? Christ's message was that He came to be the Servant, and not to be the one served. A person will have a hard time being self involved if that person is trying to serve someone else. Serving someone else takes us out of ourselves.

What is the service that lay people can do in exemplifying Christ in their lives. He cheered up his friends, He comforted them when they were afraid, He treated those who felt shame with dignity, He fed the hungry, He comforted and healed the sick, He alleviated guilt thru forgiveness, He cast out demons, He confronted hypocrisy, He defended the weak against injustice, He confronted the establishment to live up to their ideals, He taught how to pray, He taught how to live.

The Gospel talks about his judgment, "...whatsoever you do unto the least among you, you do unto Me." So He has stated He will judge you on how you treated those among you. Among you at church, at school, at work, at play, wherever you carry out your life.

Christ's whole life is a lesson on what it is to be the ideal human being, and it is a very compelling one at that. His admonishment was to spread the Good News. Carry the message that people deserve to be treated with dignity and respect, that they should rise above self pity and confront injustice, out of their ignorance learn who they are, because God is their Father, that their heritage in their nature is God-like.

Go and search out the unhealthy and the afflicted. If you have a problem serving, fake it. I was told fake it until you make it. Act your way into a new way of thinking. From a shared experience among those you treat, will come compassion. Action is the manifestation of what is in your heart. So the lay people who were amateurs, who did things for the love it, know that in doing so they will walk their talk. They will demonstrate their belief in the message of Christ by serving. Show Him, what is in your heart, where you carry out your lives.

In the course of living there are people who show up on casualty lists, so speak. The lay person will have the best opportunity to show up on the scene before any cosmetic improvements can be applied. By being a caring and loving individual, the lay person can be a messenger of hope. Many times the lay person will have been a victim of some of the same tragedies that occur. Their presence can be a message that things can and will get better, but the key is action.

They can tell the emotional cripple to get up and walk, you have that ability to walk, you have the ability to help yourself. They can tell those who are blind to their affliction, to look at it, because they have the ability to see. Stop denial, deal with the affliction by getting help.

They can demonstrate that which is vital to transformation and change in a person: the honesty to see the condition of their life, that it may need improvement, because they simply deserve better; the humility to recognize that changes are necessary, because the patterns they follow currently are harmful; enthusiasm, helping others has given them passion for life, it is contagious if you come in contact with it.

Someone who has overdosed needs to be kept in movement or they will die. The theory is to get the metabolism up to process toxins out the system. It is the same with someone overdosed on apathy, learned helplessness, ignorance, and self delusion. Get them up and moving to process the toxins of malaise, apathy, self pity, and dishonesty. If nothing else serve as an example.

In all humility I thank you for allowing me to share."

The Rollo demonstrated one of the promises of the Fellowship I belong to, that states "we will see how our experience can benefit others". Nothing in our previous experience is insignificant, everything we bring to a fellowship or a community, has the potential for helping someone achieve spiritual awakening. The two types of fellowship focus on healing.

At the heart of our discourse was the eventual development of a way for Indians to recover human dignity. Early on in our search, John had made a heartfelt plea, "Lets show our people how to be good Human Beings!" Nothing else we can think of, could be a finer goal for our efforts. From the beginning, before there emerged any structure or plan, we wanted to revive the Indian activities related to spirituality and religious practice.

There is a solid cadre of people very familiar with conducting a Cursillo. Because it is almost impossible to get the rest of the people on the reservation to one, we feel the remainder will be susceptible to Indian ceremonies. We have examined the possibilities of taking Indian ceremonies and initiating an encounter very much like the Cursillo. Once the encounter is concluded, develop a maintenance process. This is a follow-up much like the Altreya or the Twelve Step meetings. The members of this fellowship would conduct Sweats, communities of sharing, dances, and encouraging members to commit to a Vision Quest. And finally, in what we believe will be most helpful to the members, personal participation in a Vision Quest, a meeting with the True Self. What we will have is an individual searching for dignity, alone on the mountain top.

Revisiting Smowholla

The Indian ways practiced by our ancestors were developed for good practical reasons. Because the people survived, it is also reasonable to expect that the cultural practices were here for centuries.

Many people don't realize that there were a plethora of prophets and visionaries in the last century, among the local tribes. A common theme among their preachings was to maintain the Indian ways. Indian ways referred to here are the religious practices, the beliefs, and ceremonies associated with the religions.

The sweat house practices, Talking Circles, the vision quests, the chinook dances, give-aways, naming ceremonies, and the seven drums dance-ceremony, are experiencing a revival among the descendants of the local tribes. Many Indians are returning to these practices to compliment the Christian spirituality. There are other theologies and practices, notably the Twelve-Step self help programs, which emphasize the spiritual remedy to soul sicknesses. The adherents of these religions and spiritual practices, that are Indian, are looking to fill the void that still exists within themselves. The void is created by the attitude of some of the non-Indians, there is still the racism.

Those involved in the Christian and other spiritual practices keep hearing the call and feeling the beckoning from the Indian religious practices. Those who have went back and tried the ceremonies have experienced a sort of a homecoming. Why is this the case? Many of them were convinced they were fulfilled by their current spirituality. These involved in the revivals have expressed the sentiments that they belonged in those ceremonies. Active participation and personal involvement, felt most appropriate. From a disciplined point of view it seems strange and paradoxical that some people practice the ancient religions right along side their Christianity without any internal conflict.

It is hard to argue with one's intuition that the individual is in the right place, at the right time, doing the right thing.

Some have thought without overtly expressing it, that their Spiritual Guidance is directing them to turn towards these practices. Praying, meditating, blessing, worshipping, placing a total reliance on God are the common ingredients of the Christianity and the revived Indian religious practices. Quillen Chuten, the red aspect of God, of Yahweh, of Allah, or other "One" gods, beckons, and to the Indian it may be irresistable.

Warrior Transition

Spirituality is the basis of the changes in people. It is the goal of the Vision Quest, the Sweat House Ceremony, the Talking Circle or community of sharing, the dances, the giveaways. Spirituality is the building up in ourselves the godlike qualities that allows us to transcend ourselves, by doing so we achieve a close union with the god of our understanding.

Some of the things an explorer of the possibilities should consider: A reverence for life; love and compassion; the sanctity of the individual; paradox in life as a basis for meditation; true pride and true humility; forgiveness; prayer as a routine of living; ceremonies that address the needs of our spiritual nature; the stages of living in a good human being; total surrender of the self to God; all of these are matters that concern the inner life of a person.

The search for dignity is a change from a selfish, self-centered existence, to one of discipline and dedication to growth. A person who is serious in one's own mind about the search, will awaken to a new personal identity. It helps to have a self image that will inspire and encourage action in a person on such a serious endeavor. This image of action is the warrior. In our case it can be a man or a woman. It is all important to a person in the early stages of developing self regard and self respect.

Warriors of the People
Warriors have been missing from our society for a while now. They are only found in the myths and legends of our people. These are the people who protected our land, people, our ways, and ideals. They did this freely and voluntarily, with honor.

The warriors from times past learned from their parents, elders, the leaders, and medicine people, who were warriors themselves. They had the warrior's heart and soul. Their

bravery, fierceness and loyalty provided security, stability, and continuity.

We face the greatest menace to ourselves since we've been in this world as a people. Without the warriors we are a defeated and shamed people. It is because of this humiliation and shame, we are a people without honor and dignity. If there was a time we needed the warrior to save us, it is now. It is now that we must call forth the warrior from within ourselves.

This person will seek dignity and honor for the people. This person must have the courage to confront our people. Confront them with the fact that they have no vision, that they have forgotten their ideals. This person is a human being of integrity, of the highest order. This person will be humble to the extreme, and will serve in gratitude. This person will make the supreme effort, in service of the people. This person will above all love the life, he or she has made a covenant to serve.

The great warriors would serve best if they ruled within themselves the instincts that help them survive. The warrior's greatest challenge was in knowing the self; through this knowledge, develop the discipline to overcome selfishness, self-centeredness, self-pity, and self-deception. The warrior will overcome his or her own propensity for self indulgence.

The warrior will develop toughness, strength, and purity in mind and body. The warrior will reserve the highest honor and respect for the truth. The warrior will not deny or fear facing truth, for it is through truth comes knowledge of the higher purpose in life.

In all ways, constantly and vigilantly, the warrior will seek to know the higher purpose in life. It is through prayer, singing, fasting, and dancing, the warrior readies the self to receive knowledge of the higher purpose.

Who or what is this greatest menace our people have ever faced? Why is it that our people are humiliated and shamed? What has caused such incomprehensible demoralization? It is ourselves, it is those of us who have

surrendered, who are captive and prisoners to selfishness, self-centeredness, self-pity, and self-deception! It is those among us who have quit seeking their higher purpose!
Let's campaign to free our captives and prisoners.

In a previous comment or question, we asked ourselves what is the new pattern or model for our people to use in directing their lives. The warrior principle will be one of them. It is well suited for young people and people beginning on the path to spiritual growth. There are various models we can use in the different phases of person's life.

We have suspected that even those that suffered the worst from the racism would be able to respect the warrior. It wasn't something a person achieved in life automatically, it was gained as a reward after tests of character. So there was preparation and training, this suggests that there was discipline.

In Carlos Casteneda's "The Teachings of Don Juan", the Way of the Warrior was on the path on the way to the Way of Knowledge. One couldn't achieve the Way of Knowledge without first coming through the Way of the Warrior.

It is interesting that in Don Juan's way of teaching, the warriors most formidable opponents were time and the warriors own self. In the ways of personal conduct, the warrior had to actively seek a worthy opponent, and to prove oneself as a worthy opponent. A prerequisite for being a warrior was accepting the warriors condition. This acceptance is tantamount to surrendering the ego, a requirement for rebirth and transformation in most spiritual practices.

In most teachings about the Way of the Warrior, there is great importance for the warrior to overcome the self. In the way taught by Don Juan, the warrior had to overcome the propensity for self indulgence. In our local society the self indulgence comes in the form of various compulsive behaviors. We can look at sex, gambling, alcohol, drugs, pursuit of possessions, and even work. The way of the warrior provides a framework or a discipline to work on these self indulgences.

The Twelve Step programs present us with a model that works for everyone. The adherents to this program say it isn't for everybody, just those who want it. The first order of change than is the desire to become different than we are in our current condition. We can't recognize a change is in order until we see reality for what it is. A universal principle is that "the Truth will set you free". We have to want to take a look at ourselves realistically. When we see ourselves, we want to interpret our view honestly with a high regard for reality. When we see something of ourselves that is not consistant with our ego vision of who we are, we have to avoid denying reality, and accept ourselves for what we are in reality.

So when we have seen ourselves, we need the humility also to accept ourselves and recognize truthfully the necessary changes. Seeing ourselves for what we are, and become willing to make changes, comes from seeing the truth of ourselves, we will be truly set free, when this happens. These are formidable and difficult challenges to any human being, requiring the warriors attitude.

The beginning of dignity will be the recognition that we are not losers, that we are not failures in life. Somewhere along the line the individual will realize that they are not inadequate or inferior as society has made them feel. The loneliness of our existance will be diminished as we look and see that others have suffered the same humiliation and degradation as we have.

Training, discipline, sacrifice, and belief, have been mentioned as prerequisites of a warrior. Universally in tribal societies this has been the tradition of the warrior. Training basically means practicing the humility, honesty, and generosity necessary to overcome the propensity for self indulgence. Acquiring these ideals as a matter of habit. Discipline means forcing ourselves into the changes, facing the sense of futility and impatience within ourselves, and persevering. Belief means focusing our intent on changing our mindset to trust that what we do has great significance.

Growth will be the key to individuals maintaining the path undertaken for acquiring dignity. This is the path that begins the way to becoming a good human being. Key to growth is to make oneself available to a small group of fellow aspirants on this path. An individual will have to surrender the individual self centered drive for status and prestige for group or community development. The need to help others will have to replace the survival instincts that we have developed over the years just to stay alive.

In this group of fellow adherents, on the path of the warrior, one will have the opportunity to practice the compassion, sharing and caring, and surrendering the ego to a higher purpose. Many of our people have lived a life of self imposed isolation, and need to be brought gently into a community. This group or community has to break down the defensive walls and barriers individuals have erected around themselves over the years. Loving compassionate understanding as well as great patience is what will heal the isolation and loneliness of people starting on this spiritual path. Somewhere we have to recognize that in making ourselves well in spirit makes our people move in the general direction of wellness and well being as a whole. The whole process will become a communion of sorts.

Some will misconstrue the warrior principle as the standard of power and strength used in a violent manner. In our case we will try to use it as a base for security to develope a healthy sense of who we really are.

Pride in the individual will have to be replaced by pride in the group or community. The warriors will come to see that they are really one at their heart, one in spirit, one with the Creator.

Higher Purpose

Our people were fishers, hunters, and gatherers. They reverenced the land, the water, and the salmon. They knew and respected the Power that flowed thru the land, water, and the salmon, and kept our people in good fortune, and good health. They sang, danced, and prayed in honor and with love of that Power.

Newcomers came and we warred with them, and we were defeated. We were removed from our land and lumped with others into a Confederation. The Newcomers wouldn't go away. We mixed with the Newcomers and became owners of the land and forgot the Power. We mixed with Newcomers and forgot our songs, dances, stories, and prayers. The Power that kept us in good health and good fortune no longer heard us. There became more of us, but we were incomplete.

I was a slave and a prisoner. I was a man without honor and dignity. I was a liar, a cheat, and a thief. The worst thing a man could say to another was "You're chicken-shit", and they said that to me with impunity. I did not even know I was incomplete.

The Power that was ignored said "It is time to become free, time to be a man". And I was thrown out of my prison where I didn't have to think or act for myself. I was invisible to everyone, and still acted like a slave and prisoner. Again the Power said, "It is time to be free and to be a man".

In time thru talking and listening to the Power, I became free and I became a man. I was shown how to drop the ways of a slave and a prisoner. Now I walk with pride, humility, and dignity, knowing I walk as the Power showed me.

Among the Okanagon, Chelan, Methow, Wenatchee, Entiat, San Poil, Nespelem, Colville, Moses, Lakes, Nez Perce; there are many who are still slaves and prisoners.

According to the Power it is urgent to show them how to be free and to be human.

I asked the Power "Do we free them so they can sing, dance, and talk to You?" And the Power replied, "You show them how to be free and to be human, because they deserve to be! No person was created to be a slave and a prisoner! They will sing and dance, and talk with me because that is how they will learn."

I asked the Power, "What do I do about those that prefer the slavery and the way of the prisoner?" And the Power replied, "They are ignorant, you will show them how to sing, dance and to pray. They are important to you, if you don't show them, you, yourself will go back to the ways of the slave and prisoner!"

The Power told me also "I don't send you out alone, always there have been others like you, who were once slaves and prisoners. I have shown them also, and I've talked to them. I have enlightened you, as I've enlightened them, with the ways of a Good Human Being, and the ways of the Warrior. Start now, because this is your higher purpose."

The duty and responsibility is from the individual towards the group (family, band, tribe) survival. A person experiencing transformation, will undoubtably change from being a taker to a giver. The warrior principle was one of being a provider, nurturer, and a protector. The discipline inherent with duty is learned through practice, until it becomes a habit. The concern for our fellows is the most obvious sign of a transformed individual. The starting paragraph is good for a meditation in duty, discipline, and service, to our fellows. The metaphor of the slave and prisoner is most applicable to victims of racism. We have been conditioned to a mindset that cripples us spiritually and mentally. Removing the shackles that bind us, means changing our view of who we are. If we don't many will continue to act as though they are still enslaved. There can be no dignity without freedom. There is a wise saying in the Twelve Step Fellowship that says "Skid row is in our minds". The freedom we need is that which starts in our attitude and awareness of who we are. We no longer need to abide by an axiom that says we are inferior, if we believe otherwise.

Over the long term is a goal of being free to be ourselves. We can tell the truth of our own story, and not listen to the story line of our inferiority. We can appreciate the meaning that we are good enough the way we are. The other possibility is that we will free ourselves of hatred and resentment that prevents us from becoming the good human being.

In our quest for dignity we can recognize the false stories about our ancestors. With a sense of destiny, we can develop a new true history for ourselves. We can reestablish the continuity with our forefathers that all Americans claim a right to. Again we can take pride in the fact our people were good. We can take a sense of vindication in the knowledge that "pagans" and "savages" are but lables whose source is ignorance, fear, and intolerance.

The lables that have been put on us are a form of oppression. The higher purpose of gaining human dignity, means confronting this oppression. A large part of this oppression is that we let the attitudes of intolerance and bigotry govern our existance. We must confront this because there are principles held dear to everyone that we, "are vested by our Creator with certain inalienable rights". In this process we should confront the society we live in that they do not live up to their ideals. Much of the problems of society stem from the fact that we all have strayed from the fact that the Creator has vested us with life. We forget to be humble. We all have forgotten to look at our basic intrinsic value to the Creator.

There will come an understanding about of much of our experience that we may have considered insane. The rage we knew was there, that would surface at the most inopportune moments. Our inability to seek redress from slights, because the energy of the response was too intense for one such incident, built up from many such incidents. There seemed to be no middle ground. Everything that dealt with our emotions was borderline hysteria. As we share many of these with our fellows, they will no longer cause us shame. Sharing will humanize us, a process highly necessary for the dehumanization we've gone through.

When one takes up this meditation seriously, we achieve an awareness that a major portion of our purpose here is to help one another, to take care of each other. Basically each of us must learn to love each other, giving each other spiritual sustenance. We have to come to the realization that the well being and health of the community or group, means our own individual well being and health.

A higher purpose for a people will change the selfish materialistic approach that has been part of the enslavement of our people. We have been hypnotized into thinking that road to becoming a good human being means acquiring things, and gaining status and prestige for ourselves individually. The fact that we even start to put others before ourselves will start the process of change we desire.

The higher purpose represents a basic human need, that is to belong to something greater than ourselves. There has to be something in our lives that will motivate us to exceptional achievement. In the popular business press there is a term called "synergism" in high usage. The fact that we are looking out for the good of a group, and trying to change basic values and beliefs for the greater good, will synergyze us. We will engergize each other by the simple fact that we share with each other. A higher purpose will guide our lives over the long term, it will provide us with a vision for our community.

Much of what we will learn early on will be through a group or fellowship. For the majority of us, the Creator will communicate to us through other people. The Twelve Step program talks about spiritual awakenings for the most of us will be educational. Education is drawn from a Greek word whose root meaning is derived from "a drawing out of". What this implies is that there is already something there worthwhile. In a group we can draw out the best in each other. From our experience we can draw out a vision for all of us that will be uplifting. We can by interacting with each other, set our sights on higher standards of moral and ethical values.

If we get to the heart of our being, we can find that there is honor and nobility within all of us. Right now, for many, there is but a thirst, that we don't know how to quench. Many of us are only vaguely aware that we strive for integrity naturally, but we've been diverted, and our purpose in life perverted by the indoctrination of inferiority. Our higher purpose is to get off the floor and stand on our own. We need to provide ourselves with the respect and dignity we deserve.

The Creator becomes the teacher, the care-giver, the source of wisdom, the miracle maker of our transformation. Much of what we will learn early on will be through a group or fellowship. For the majority of us, the Creator will communicate to us through other people.

This meditation can become a framework of a common purpose and a guide to sharing. The habitual use of this meditation will bring the individual to the important goals in life, to be useful to the Creator and fellows, to acquire a discipline, to be useful.

It is good to remind ourselves that progress and growth are necessary for groups as well as individuals. If groups develop some internal conflicts, and are not resolved the group will dissolve. The Talking Circle is a good vehicle to conduct the reviews and debriefing on growth and challenges confronting individuals. It would be the place to disclose the personal discoveries of the sweat and of the fast. For unity in a community the Talking Circle is the core. It contains the ground rules that allow us to deal with jealousy and criticism. The Talking Circle has inherently the rules for respectful listening, this is a skill largely still missing in the community.

The unity of community is where the individuals will feel empowered to change their lives for the better. In the talks between the members, one will hear the word of the Creator through the voices of other participants. Somehow the wisdom emerges, answers to life's more complex questions come to us at the most serendipitous time. The twelve step groups have what is called a group conscience that make the critical decisions that effect the group. This emerges after a person learns to listen respectfully. Listening respectfully, means that every person participating has something of value and worth to contribute. Nothing said in a Talking Circle is insignificant. Nothing in our lives is insignificant.

Carriers of Wisdom

The young people, warriors, our leaders, and elders all need to turn to the wisdom of our people at one time or the other. Wisdom is one of those intangible things, you know when you're in its presence, but you are at a loss to describe it. The description is elusive as the spirits, yet tangibly felt in the warmth and comfort of fellowship.

It is of the people, it comes from within the people, still with us through the ages. It is the soulful heartfelt learning applied to all our experiences from our collective memories. It is an aspect of the soul, best understood as a knowing-feeling.

We draw on it thru meditation and prayer, as such it is an article of faith. The acquisition of wisdom is the process of a spiritual journey, it is not the destination. It comes to us in enlightenment, insight, and inspiration. It is our Maker's message telling us where to look inside ourselves to find answers and solutions to challenges. Since part of it is from the Maker, it is by the grace of the Maker, we get it. It is partly gift, partly reward.

Wisdom will be communicated only through the humility and honesty of the carrier. Humility is recognition that by the grace of the Maker you have received a gift. Honesty is the individual's most profound and eloquent understanding and interpretation of reality. As the individual's most eloquent and profound understanding and interpretation, it comes from the deepest part of the individual.

Wisdom by its nature is both individualistic and a collective or group endeavor. A person or a community, honestly and humbly, adopt an attitude of expectation, respect, and reverence, to examine experience and memory meditatively. The knowledge of right or wrong are related to new experience, memory, and feeling. This process involves both the mind and the heart, our knowing and feeling parts of ourselves.

Since it is knowing-feeling it is best communicated in ceremony and rite. Dances, songs, art, myths-stories, and other interpretations of beauty, will convey to the young, our warriors, our leaders, and our elders the wisdom of our people. It is brought out by a community of wise-individuals, who prepare themselves to be receivers of wisdom. It is those who open themselves to the beauty and wonder of our world through their own sense of awe, wonder, and reverence, who will develop the knowing-feeling.

We are going to have people filling the elder's roles who are going to be convinced they can't be elders. This meditation directs one to the attitude to adopt in accessing wisdom within ourselves, that we normally don't think we possess. Much is there if our approach is prayerful and reverent. Some of it will come from the Creator, or your Higher Power, some will come from our own unconscious selves.

What a person feels about reality is very much dependant on how that person views the individual self in relationship to the community, the environment, and to the Creator. The first and paramount idea of a new self image is that as an individual you're good enough the way you are naturally. Remember and recognize the godliness of your nature. If you could hear the Creator singing you would hear, "you are -so beautiful, - - to Me!", (repeated three times) maybe even in Joe Cocker's voice.

The image of the self is composed by the self and should only be changed by the self. Recognition that you are more than the ego, that the real self is much deeper and profound, makes for stability and consistency in our self awareness. If you value yourself, or love yourself less than is good for you, your self image will be changed from the outside. Generally suggested changes of your image from the outside are denigrating.

I have always struggled with the idea that I wasn't good enough. Even when I accomplished or achieved something significant, there was always this thing lurking in the back my mind, that it wasn't quite good enough. I've suffered from this obsessive compulsion to be working and doing. A restlessness and dis-ease are components of this phenomena I share with many Indians. A common mistake we all made is to compare our insides with the outsides of others.

The indoctrination that I was inferior followed me everywhere I went in life. In school, in the military, at work, and in church, was a reminder always, "You're Indian, and you're not as valued as the rest of us." It is noteworthy that consistent with this notion of inferiority, was a distancing or removing myself away from God. It is through God comes our true understanding of who we are in reality.

The healthy and wholesome self images are rooted in one's relatedness to God. We are individual expressions of God, and that through us, God will experience Creation as only we, as individuals could. We have the sentiment that we are made in the image and likeness of God. Our very essence is that of God. Our character and nature than is spiritual. We are creators, healers, teachers, care-givers, protectors, forgivers, explorers, nurturers, in every sense that God is such.

In the development of such a self image, it is preponderant on ourselves to help foster such an image in others. If we are to mirror God, how could we want anything less than the best for others. This self image has to be tempered with humility, the recognition that others possess this same God-mirroring nature. We should celebrate with them this common bond.

There are remnants of the teachings held dear to our people, in the memories of various individuals living around the reservation. When we put these together we see a structure and order to the way our people conducted themselves spiritually before the changes we have been discussing occured.

The various fragments are in the stories, myths and legends, people somehow have retained. There vague memories of ceremonies conducted in longhouses, sweats, and dances. Implicit in all of these is the idea that we are just part of the whole. There are no stories or legends that tell us we were "Lords of the forest". That we were to conquer the wilderness and subjugate all living things, wasn't part of our make-up.

The ownership of the land was as farfetched to the first

124

inhabitants of this land, as was owning the sunlight. We were part of the earth just as the water and air, plants, and animals. All of these had spirit, all of these had life. Within this framework we had our place, we had responsibility, we did not have dominance.

As we grow out of our ignorance we find out that we have an idea of who we are basically. We are caretakers in a sense. We been indoctrinated otherwise. Part of our newly acquired understanding of who we are, is that we can choose what goes around in our thoughts and the feelings we experience and express. This is part of our new responsibility. We have to rule within our own minds, because as we think, so we become.

These awesome gifts shared by all human beings, must be used and exercised. They must be developed to a high degree. The creative nature has to be such as to emulate the Creator. We need to love, as the Creator has loved. Mostly we need to learn from the painful lessons of the past and those emerging from the present. We have a responsibility to exercise our freedoms we claim as human beings.

The wise elders seem to tell us, make choices and see what you will find out for yourself. Experience life to its fullest, that is what creation is all about. At our basic fundmental nature is this spiritual being particapating in Creation. For now we have a hunch that this is way things are. We have a feeling that there is great meaning and significance to existance that we will have to explore and discover ourselves. Our intuition tells us that we are surrounded by mystery, that if we search and probe we will achieve enlightenment.

How do we get to the searching, many feel we must undertake, if we are focused in hatred, fear, and self preservation? Much of it is developing a sense of awe for the creation in which we live, appreciate the greaty beauty on display. Develope a sense that it is miraculous that such a thing has even occured. We have restricted ourselves so severely in our experience, many forget that the restrictions are self imposed limitations.

We but have to open our minds and hearts to the possibilities. Let us open our hearts to the possibility of the presence of the Creator within us, within others. Let us find a way to conceive of the possibility that we are spiritual beings first. We start by being aware that we already know. We start by getting to that real self, that part of ourselves we all share as one with the Creator.

Preparation to Meet our True Selves

Finding instruction to conduct a vision quest locally is a predicament. We have people who talk about the process, but don't treat it with the seriousness that it deserves. It is here we will consider what the first quester did to succeed.

The first person to undertake such a quest we are talking about, had to do so as an explorer and an experimenter. All persons undertaking a quest in our age must have the courage and the curiosity of an explorer, an adventurer, or experimenter. The first person then, probably undertook much praying and meditating, through which was explored the many paths of spirituality. Close attention to dreams and their content was paid, the first person in all likelihood received direction from here. An awareness that dreams are the spirit's communication to us is a development each quester should seek to acquire.

The people who have been on vision quests have stated that the experience is different for everyone. So we are looking at variations and possibilities as variable as there are individuals.

There is nothing so fulfilling as the discovery of one's self as a worthwhile human being. This is what we strive to induce in the people.

So we must treat our activity with all the respect it is due. We must understand what we do is very serious. We must know that we are undertaking what is by far the noblest adventure of our lives. We should approach this activity as if we were preparing ourselves to meet a great and important chief.

A prerequisite for anyone undertaking a quest, is a high regard or reverence for honesty. Sometimes changes and transformations in a person are disorienting or destablizing. We must acquire an understanding with our inner-most selves that we are undertaking this quest in search for dignity. We are in search of health and wholesomeness we admit is missing in our own lives. It is most helpful for us to acknowledge that the way we previously have been conducting our lives, based on our values and beliefs, has been detrimental to our spiritual health and well being.

We then must realize that a spiritual process is required to make it possible to acquire dignity. We must acknowledge and recognize whole-heartedly that we must rely on a Spiritual Guidance in this quest, and that without this Spiritual Guidance we are powerless. We gain access to this Guidance through prayer and meditation, generally with assistance from a person who may have more experienced in the search.

At some point in time we must commit totally to making the best effort we can muster in our search. We must commit to being as honest as we can be. We must commit to being as selfless as can be, and have the most willingness we can bring out of ourselves to be teachable. Humility is the key, we must recognize that we are powerless without our Spiritual Guidance. In our humility we must recognize that our limited growth, limited our awareness. We must totally and willingly, be ready to receive new types of awareness, new information about reality, in ways that are unfamiliar to us.

As a recognition of the times we live in, writing will be introduced into the process. A list of the quester's good and bad qualities is developed, so the person knows wholeheartedly what they bring to the Spiritual Guidance, and what needs to be changed. In this listing is a candid and honest evaluation of one's fears, resentments, jealousies, and lack of tolerance towards others. Included in this list is the good qualities a person brings to help the self complete the quest.

Acceptance of the fact that when a person conducts a successful quest that the quester is changed irreversibly. After the search the quester will be entirely different in one's view of reality, of personal values and beliefs. The quester must be totally aware that the undertaking of a vision quest leads to a rebirth of the person. As was already discussed, the quester meets the Real Self.

All the time during this process the quester will share experience, strength, and expectations with someone who has accomplished the endeavor. This person will prepare the questor for what will actually occur during the quest.

A person preparing for such an endeavor as we are discussing needs some encouragement, and affirmation. So the members of this reservation will in all likelihood look to Indians from other tribes to help in preparation.

Purification before conducting a quest was a common practice of our aboriginal ancestors. It also should be remembered that vision quests were once also a common practice. Much of what we're are considering was a matter of hygiene to our forebears as is our showering, shaving, and brushing our teeth. Their hygienic practices were holistic and were directed as much towards spiritual purification as with personal cleanliness.

The spiritual purification meant the elimination of a bad heart, or intentions on the part of the quester. This could be hatred, anger, jealousy, envy, indecisiveness, and fear, directed towards someone else or oneself. Another example is a low opinion or bad judgement directed towards another person. It is important to remove this opinion and the act of judging another, prior to the quest. Ulterior motives must be removed. Things like undertaking the quest for personal aggrandizement, or for the sake of one's public image, to show off, or as a way of putting down another.

The fears of a person must always be addressed in purification. Misdirected fear must be alleviated and corrected. The quester must be enlightened on fear of the practice, and fear of the unknown. We should instruct the individual to fear the known by which he or she is seriously constrained and enslaved. The Unknown is our route to unlimited possibilities. Faith in the consequences of spiritual practices is a growth process that marks the readiness of the individual.

Much of the activity discussed is done in conjunction with the sweat ceremony. The sweat ceremony is the way for the quester to pray and meditate. In the sweat the quester is purified. In the sweat the quester receives the strength and courage to undertake the actual quest. In the sweat, during meditation, The quester receives the knowledge that they are ready.

The Quest

The Vision Quest, this is the most intriguing element of our most recent enlightenment. Here we will confront our fears, hatreds, emptiness, phobias, and whatever we hide in our innermost selves. As George and Melvin have indicated, this is how we will meet our true selves. That in itself makes it exciting enough to overshadow the challenges that make us reluctant to get on with one. John has stated that if we are going to be teaching or instructing anyone we'll have to have experienced what we're trying to pass on, that makes a lot of sense.

Something like this will be a means to discipline the more boisterous and energetic individuals. The preparation and the commitment necessary is a good way to prepare a person for the commitments of life.

The deprivation of the body and mind in the fasting part of The Quest is metaphoric of the deprivation of the spirit. We have deprived our souls of much of its needed sustanence. It is through the experience of the painful deprivation of the body do we get an idea of the suffering of our spirit. For years our souls thirsted and hungered for the conscious contact with the Creator, and Great Grand-Mother, and the Grandfather.

The deprivation also gives us humility. It gives us the full meaning of the sacredness of life, how fragile is the balance of living. We develop a deeper more profound meaning of water as the source of life, a gift of the Great Grand Mother. The water we take in, the food we eat, and the air we breath, unify us with all of creation. It is this unity, or oneness we crave. It is the oneness with Creation, with our fellows, our families, with our communities, Oneness that is love.

"Shu um makh" -- "Higher Power", I've taken the liberty to make these synonymous. In the cultural tradition of our forebears, a person got this Shu um makh as the result of undertaking a vision quest. The person acquired a guide or advisor, a model for living, or an overriding direction in life, or even insight into one's personal vocation. In the acquisition of personal power, this Shu um makh gave the successful seeker a song. This song was personally empowering, encouraging, or inspiring. Other names for this Shu um Makh is ally, animal guide, animal power, because the Shu um makh will most often appear as an animal.

From experiences passed down through the elders of our contemporary community the search for a Shu um makh was deeply ingrained in the cultural practices of the local tribes. All the legends and myths that have survived tell of various people doing this in their adventure of life. Coyote went on a number of these, and he seems to have ended up with a number of "advisers".

The participant begins a spiritual and physical in isolation. Once there the individual begins a period of praying and singing, fasting, and meditation. In this fashion the individual empties his or herself of the self. The Quester waits, ready and receptive, one on one with the self, one on one and at one with God.

One on one with oneself, without the distractions of everyday living is conducive to acquiring knowledge of the self. The chatter of a person's inner dialogue has to be accounted for and quieted. At this point one can examine honestly, personal and private views of reality, beliefs and values, visions and aspirations for the future, and finally determine one overriding goal in life. Our goal is to overcome the life without dignity, pointlessness and the hopelessness of the life of alcoholism, violence, compulsive behavior, loss of self, or any type of spiritual malady.

There is the possibility that a person can't withstand the conscious contact with one's Spiritual Guidance, without a preparation of purification. The body and mind need to be cleansed and the consciousness expanded, so to speak. The changes that result can be disorienting and de-stabilizing. The preparation is usually guided by a mentor. As a person returns from a quest, a debriefing or sharing of the experience with this mentor aids in the transition.

There are in the preparation, some "practice" quests so the individual can be even better prepared for the actual quest. Some individuals start out with on day and a night, and build up to four days and nights. In this period of the actual quest, the individual is transformed.

One of the outcomes of the Vision Quest is the acquisition of a new name by the person who undertakes the venture. A new name indicates a new person or personality. This means that there is the distinct possibility that The Quest is conducive to rebirth, or spiritual awakening, hence the acquisition of a new name for the new person.

The Vision

Like most people, I made the presumption that the vision would be of the type one would see in an apparition. Each of us expects to see something outside of the ordinary world. The oral tradition of our people, or what was left of it, made it sound this way. I suspect that the translation to English is what caused this. One must question, how did the English word "vision", got into the term "Vision Quest". Is what the Indian term describes, mean the same thing? Is there some distortion of what is meant originally, much of it making for a narrow or restricted translation. This inability to translate indicates a rich spiritual heritage of our ancestors. The narrow translation is another indication of the inferiority projected on our people and our culture.

There have been movies and books about non-Indians making a serious effort to find their place in life. Some of it is about these individual finding out who they are. As a universal principle, people intuitively comprehend what it is. Everyone uses it as the same spiritual metaphor. But limitations of the English language to describe the reality of the heart and soul probably leave us with this term. Although limited and narrow, is so far the best description of what we are trying to achieve.

Each person will have or find their vision if they maintain an open heart and an open mind. There are mystics and visionaries who have the sort of visions we have in mind. And people want to see these fantastic scenes as proof of the validity, of what we want to do in a fast or vision quest. Commitment requires that we reach the point in our spiritual growth and development that we achieve the vision aspect.

An association game with the word vision will broaden our meaning and the possibilities latent in our activities. The first thing to come to mind is "seeing". What comes to mind immediately is images on the mind from what we see with our eyes. There are also images in our mind when we envision a goal we want to achieve. What exactly are the images we see in our sleeping dreams. And in some cases when we realize that we are dreaming, who is doing the seeing? We develop seeing in terms of our ideals for our fellows, as members of a society or community. Our values and beliefs create an ideal for what we see as the best community we can have.

Our seeing can differentiate between the ideals and the current reality. And then there is the seeing when we can "see" what another person feels or aspires to. This type of seeing is the hunch type, a "knowing feeling" associated with one's intuition. The seeing in this aspect crosses over into the acquisition of knowledge or wisdom. When we get into the word "know", we get into the meaning when we refer to what best describes speaking or hearing from the heart. There is an aspect of perception that is intuitional. We have hunches that sometimes lead us to make decisions that we just "know" are right and correct for us. This comes from a "little voice", all of us can hear it , but to which too few listen.

Another word that comes to mind when we associate with "vision" is perception. This is loaded with meaning for what we understand intellectually or pick up from our environment with our physical senses. It might be that keen development of our physical senses leads into development of a sixth sense. Hunters have all talked about a time in their lives when they feel or know the presence of their quarry.

Not only do we understand now, but we have a capacity for newer understanding to build on what we already perceive or know.

Our leaders are supposed to have "super-vision". We expect that they will "see" what those led, envision for society, and by a process of analysis and synthesis, develop a vision for society that will motivate those led. From the communication of the leader, those being led receive the vision of society by the leader. It is from being able to see where the vision has failed to take into account what every individuals needs, that this effort at looking at visions was started.

The failure comes from the leadership not being able to

"know" what the individuals needs are. There are many those who can't communicate their needs, or are so completely lost that to just say what is best is beyond them. These are the ones who need the leadership supervision most urgently. These are the ones who have somehow missed the ideals, beliefs, and values of society. It is our contention they have been excluded from society, while the alternatives have been obliterated. In many cases it is the inability of many of our leadership to see or hear with heart.

Martin Luther King's speech of "I have a dream", best describes what a person will acquire in their individual quests. Mr. Kings dream for Americans, was his vision. His vision was derived from his super-vision of those he led. In many ways his ideals speak for all peoples who were excluded from the American Dream. His vision was rooted in his ability to see that we all are God's children. His vision was motivated by his perception that we needed to be one as a nation, as a people. This need to be one as a people in a unity, is love. This adds another aspect to our perception or what we see or know.

Another association is ideals. As we reference ideal we look at what are the best possibilities for ourselves. We try to understand or know what our potential is for perfection or excellence. We want people to understand that at the root of their essential nature, is their image and likeness to divinity. At some point in time we think people will come to believe and understand that by nature, they are creators. They must know that it is they who create the reality they experience. In the mysterious ways of creation, we can create meaning from our tragic existence, during the last one hundred years. This is one of the more beautiful aspects of the meaning of vision.

It is the vision and belief in the validity of that vision that traps much of our less fortunate tribal members. They have come to believe that they are inferior. And because this belief has so much reinforcement from continual conditioning, it carries powerful apparent validity, and appears as a vision to be unassailable. To help our people we will assault this belief, and change the very reality that traps many of our people.

The world of impoverishment, not only materially but

spiritually is the vision of many of our people. They seem to be entranced by it. The awakening is receiving or acquiring the ability to see the world as it really is, we want to bring this to our people. This awakening will help to break the spell that holds many a prisoner to the world of alcoholism, gambling, violence, and poverty.

The vision we want to instill has always been available to all of us. The disruption of our cultural activities and the destruction of our language has done much to destroy the vision our people had of themselves. This loss is the what many are grieving for, it is the source of our incompleteness. Our journey to completeness and wholesomeness begins, as William James tells us, with prayer.

We need to acquire a vision or perception of our intrinsic worth. Our vision of our value collectively and individually, for many without dignity, has been extrinsic at it source. A vision of who we are, and our sense of a lack of self-value, has been imposed from the outside. The change must start from the inside.

In many ways this means changing the emphasis of our reality, from an objective impoverished reality, to a subjective reality. We must change our vision of ourselves from being observers and reactors to being the Human Beings we are. Being is composed of both types of reality. Being is state and an activity, we must experience this in the our vision of reality. Being that our nature is by image and likeness divine, it isn't constrained to time and physicalness.

Being as we are describing it, brings with it some universal principles that can be applied to all people. All people who pray, acknowledge their dependance on a Spiritual Being. All people have ceremonies composed of prayers to this Spiritual Being. All people have fasting in their repretoir of prayers and ceremonies. All people have journeys to isolation to be alone to pray. A combination of these is what the quest for our people is.

The awesome beauty of the world is taken for granted. Many people drink water and take food very casually without realizing the significance to our very existence of these things. The fast and the quest bring us to the realization of the sacred quality of water, food, and air. Our vision of our existence is enhanced from our experience in fasting. We come to see our unity with creation, how much natural harmony balance there already is. To see this is a broadening of our perception or acquisition of a vision. We see the blessedness of our natural world. We see the rightness or balance, or as many would say the grace, that is inherent in creation.

Many of us are ignorant of the dynamic complexity of what makes up our being and our experience of reality. Some might be intimidated by what is hinted at here, but much of it flows naturally as a consequence of a relationship with the Creator. Our guidance when we need it, will come in the form of healing, inspiration, and insight. Our trust in life will motivate us to act to make the necessary changes in our vision, if we are trapped by the indoctrination of inferiority. The acquisition of a vision of our intrinsic worth will help us "know" that we deserve better from life as Indian Peoples.

There are the images created when we are in a reveries or day dreaming. These images in our reveries need to receive a higher regard because they come from our creative capacity to imagine. What we envision guides much of our living experience. So we are guiding a rather fantastic creation without realizing what we are doing. An acquisition of a vision helps to "see" that we need to learn how to guide or direct this Being that we are with greater care and loving.

So we come full circle and back to the visions we will receive on a fast or vision quest. Many want to see animal spirits. Many want to talk with animal spirits or receive a power or healing song. Many will want to talk with the spirits and receive a new name. What many want is proof. We want to act on faith that the Creator will hear our prayers and receive our sacrifices. These other things happened to our ancestors because that was the reality they lived. Our expectations and our beliefs have to change drastically to be able to experience these in our fasting or vision quests. We are acting on our beliefs, we demonstrating our faith in the Creator when we conduct such activities. We will experience what our ancestor experienced once we let go of the constraining forces of our current beliefs.

We have to hold very strongly the beliefs in the possibilities of the fast or the quest. We have to understand that the activities we are undertaking are mystical and spiritual in nature. So it is necessary to examine our spiritual beliefs.

When we realize that we participate in the creation of our experience, we come to "know" that what we expect is what we will experience. This expectation is the beliefs we hold about reality. We need to understand our innermost beliefs to understand our experiences. It is the wonderful part about the journey to meet our "real selves". This self understanding or self awareness, is the new vision of ourselves as Being.

Our vision in the final analysis will be even more fantastic, if that is a correct way to describe it, than we had originally expected it to be. In the miraculous process we follow, growth to the proper level brings us the ability to acquire the understanding and knowledge. There are universal principles at work here, that enable us to achieve a transition in our entire being. It is no casual activity, it does require complete genuine commitment.

Like many people I was under the impression that a person did this once in their lifetime. But given the richness and complexity of life and creation, it is a lifetime activity. Once we reach a certain plateau of growth and achievement, we set our vision on the next one. It is part and parcel of our being, to be constantly ever growing and learning, becoming more and more of what the Creator intended us to be. Like much of the mysteries of life, we misunderstood the "Vision" as a destination, when in all actuality it is the journey.

Entering Into a Relationship with the Creator

The Sweat Talk

Quillen Chuten - Maker of Life - Maker of the sun - Maker of the earth - Maker of the water - Maker of the air - Maker of the deer and salmon - Maker of the camas and all roots - Maker of the berries. Because of You, I am. But for You, we live in this beautiful and awesome world, I humbly acknowledge and honor your greatness and generosity.

Quillen Chuten - Maker of my spirit - Maker of my heart - Maker of my mind - Maker of my body. Because of You, I am. But for You, I think. But for You, I feel. You made me a free person. You made me with dignity and wanted me to act as such. You made me pure. You made me with the love of a Father and Mother, because You wanted what was best for me. I recognize that I am but a child, - a child of Yours. Like a spoiled child I ignored Your goodness. You let me see and experience hell, - and let me come back. Accept my tears as now I cry for Your Comfort.

Quillen Chuten - Bringer of the Light. Show me how to be honest- Show me how to value purity in mind, body and spirit - Show me how to be the way You intended me to be. Show me how to talk to you all the time. Show me how to always, all the time, have You in my heart. Show me how to know myself. Show me how to know You.

Prayers and praying are the primary means that people make themselves healthy and wholesome. In my own life, transformation has occurred because I prayed. Prayer, according to William James in his "Varieties of Religious Experience", is the form of every individuals' personal religion. In prayer we acknowledge that our very existence is dependant on that to which we pray. It is this attitude of reverence and deep respect that helps us to transcend ourselves. During this activity we achieve a relationship with whatever we perceive as divine, part of this relationship is a union or communion.

The healing comes from this relationship with the Divine. That which was stripped from us, is returned. The validation and valuation that came from an external source, now comes from God, within ourselves. In this new relationship is revealed to us expectations from God, that we will always grow, that we will always achieve above and beyond our current capacities, that we are instruments of God. In this awareness comes our dignity. In the awareness that our very existence is dependant on the good graces of God, comes our humility. The awareness that God loves us, and would never allow us to become non-existent, gives us the awareness of our tremendous worth.

This is a meditation for someone who has evolved a personal relationship with one's god. The prayer is an affirmation of one's dependance and reliance on that Spiritual Guidance in our lives. It particularly intensifies in meaning while conducting a sweat ceremony.

Many of us begin our relationship with the Creator convinced that we are separated or apart from this source of our being. We have been indoctrinated not only with the sense that we are inferior to non-Indians, but that we are unworthy, deserving of the greatest shame. Many of us are certain there is a Creator, but this Being is busy, keeping the universe in order. Certainly this divine Being is too busy to listen to us and our problems personally.

The fact that we have distanced ourselves from the source of our life, is a choice we have exercised. The sense of need or want, a sense of incompleteness, are the effects of such a separation. As we are able to understand ourselves, we discover that we are one with the Creator. What we lack is the ability to commune with this Being, or to make some comprehensible contact. Our path to becoming a good human being, helped us acquire the belief of the Caring Creator. Much of our lives we were convinced that the Creator was unapproachable, or at the very least indifferent to our situation.

There is even part of the indoctrination of inferiority that preaches that perhaps the Creator had abandoned us. Wasn't our predicament evidence that this was the case? The suicides and self distructive life styles and habits, indicate that sense of hopelessness and futility of our existance. The sermons hinted at the possibility of being paganistic caused the demise of our culture. There is implicit in the comparison of morality, hinting that because of the difference of our peoples, we were cursed and damned. Of course we have lived with this belief for some one-hundred years.

Being a people who have had ample opportunity to hunt and fish, and to gather foods in the ways of people have done for eons, there was a remainder of a connection with the land. There was a sense of a relationship, although not nearly as close as that of our ancestors. For one thing we were brought to this land from places we had lived historically. Yet there was the respect and reverence for the life giving qualities of the land. My grandfather reminded me, "Even your fancy truck, comes from the land!"

As our enlightenment and awareness becomes fuller, so does or relationship with the Creator. This implies that we can conceive of our relatedness. There is the Creator, here is myself, we are one, yet we feel distance and separateness. The distance we feel is our moving away from the relationship. The Lakota and other plains Indians have a saying, "All my relations", to affirm our relatedness to the creation. We are one with our brothers the "Wind", the "Moon", the "Four-legged", the "Winged', and the water creatures.

As hunters there was the recognition that life was taken so that other life could continue. That which sustained deer, salmon, camas, and berries, sustained us in the web of life. In the end of our physical existance, we in turn became food for the continuation of life. As a youngster I was angered by the evil Crow for stealing young ones of other birds. I was later to understand, there is no evil, Crow was being Crow. Because we have this relationship, we can understand our place in creation.

We not only call out and say "Grandfather", we say "Great Grandmother", which indicate a strong and close relationship. The Creator than would be the giver of comfort, of nurturing, as a parent would. In our relatedness, we view ourselves as children of the Creator. Everything, our very heartbeat, our thinking ability, is the gift of the Creator. In our relationship we are the recepients of many blessings, although most of think we are destitute.

The relationship that developes in our spiritual quest, is one where the Creator is the teacher, we are the ones doing the learning. We receive enlightenment and develop insights as we participate in this relationship. In times of great challenge, we are encouraged and motivated to rise up and meet challenge as the result of asking for help. We recieve guidance to some of lifes more perplexing situations.

There is a commonality among the Indians that each person has a spirit guide or helper. The relationship is that of among friends and companions. As the person developes the individual can recall the number of times the name of the Creator or spirit guide, was called out in a mantra like fashion.

Many of our acquaintences all can testify to incidents where they should have been killed, or seriously harmed in some way. By some fluke they survived unharmed. They proclaim, "Was I lucky or what?" In our worst years we were in a one way relationship, we were takers, never sharing, never giving. We weren't lucky, we were the recipients of help and protection, whose source was the spirit.

As we grow the relationship grows, from a supplicant for just a bit of a break or rest, to particapant in creation. But it is important that we realize that it was we who created the separation that caused us the sense of dis-ease. There is great paradox, in that the we can't recognize the power of our creations, which are our beliefs in our own inadequacy. We feel terribly helpless and impotent in overcoming these beliefs. In our relationship there will be the feelings that will color the state of the ralationship. Sometimes there will be anger, followed by confusion, or perhaps fear, followed by relief. The basis of the relationship is love. All the things that people share in a relationship are possible in a relationhip with the Creator.

When we look at our interpersonal relationships we can see what occurs. We can see what to expect in our relationship with the Creator. With our parents we shared our vision and dreams for the future. We were grateful for the things they gave us in our short lives. With our brothers and sisters, we shared our discoveries through adventures and other excitment we found in life. We developed bonds and loyalties. We become devoted to those we loved. For those we were in a relationship with, we developed a sense of duty and responsibility.

The things we do in our relationships will be carried out with our Creator. We can visit, hold conversations, celebrate. We listen to those close to us. This might be the hard part for any of us. One of the abilities we sorely lack is this ability to listen and act on what we heard. We don't ignore those close to us, but we seem to do much of this with our Creator. The difficulty we face is one of obedience if we lack the humility or honesty.

So in a relationship, we can be a student, a soldier, a channel, or an instrument. We can be the messenger of this relationship. We can be the example of such a relationship. Much of this will be our choice, but also it will be the choice of those around us. What we will find is that those around us will make choices about their relatedness to us. The difficulties we experience in our relationships, is based in our inability to accept and respect the choices others make in regard to their relationship to us individually.

The prayer at the beginning of this chapter was inspired by the Sweat. As we were taught when we were young, and almost forgot, that this is where we go to ask for the things we need. We have reached a point in this relationship to have complete trust in the Other, and perhaps some trust in ourselves.

Healing

All healing is spiritual because there is no separation of the body and the soul. If there is some malady in the soul it will affect the body. Healing is a return to the original condition of the body and soul.

The things we learn of being exposed to other cultures, is helpful in understanding the words we use. "Meditation" is a good example, it is closely related to "medicine". "Salvation" is another one, it is closely related to "salve". When one listens to preachers and evangelists and we tend to hear these words with an already contrary attitude. I'm already to negate a sermon that tells me I'm bad, I just don't want to hear it. I do not want to "repent" which is another one of those misunderstood and misused words. Repent means to re-think or change your mind. All the great holy men of all time were healers, they healed the troubled hearts and sick souls. Actually they showed you how to do the good things for yourself. They preached and sermonized "Pray and meditate with your god, your salvation is in your god, repent your ways if you have a troubled heart"

In the Cursillo is a lesson given on the changing sense of sin. When a person violates internal directives or guidance, a warning is issued. When we ignore these warnings enough times, we start to tell ourselves we are bad. We distance ourselves from whatever it is we consider divine. This new sense of sin is very helpful to me. I've started to examine those internal directives. Somehow there was one in there that said, "Your ancestors were heathen and pagan, your people don't worship the right god, or worship in the right way, and by the way you are different, and bad. You are going to have to humiliate yourself before me before you can be considered good." I do not have to distance myself from God, because a strange instruction got into my internal dialogue. For years I felt that people meant sinners were synonymous with Indian.

Healing in mostly removing the causes of shame, guilt, and worry. The causes are usually a lack internal validation and valuation of ourselves, we haven't made amendments for violating ourselves and other persons by apologizing and asking forgiveness, and presuming we can control every aspect of our lives and those around us. We get back to the idea of acquiring honesty, humility, and courage. If one looks at the "Warrior of Our People", the person striving to become a warrior, was actually practicing to heal the self. Dignity although our most apparent goal, is the result of our efforts to heal ourselves and our fellows.

Sacred Ceremonies will probably be activities that will be a vehicle for an individual's prayer or praying, the means for healing. This could be the Vision Quest, the Sweat, a give-away, a Chinook Dance, the Seven Drums ceremonies, etc. These activities are transcendent and bring the individual into a conscious relationship with whatever the individual considers divine, or his/her true self. Singing is a new prayer form, for me at least. It basically will be determined by the meaning the individual brings to the ceremony.

Songs are a form of prayer and out of ignorance, I never considered them as such. When I was a child I learned hymns, which were prayers. But the songs I learned from my people, I never considered prayers. The Chinook Dance songs I learned were actually prayers for good health and good fortune. The Stick Game songs are songs that truly express the joy and affirmation of life. If they have words, I'm not aware of them, but they give full expression to one's own knowing/feeling.

Songs are sounds of power. They are expressions from that part of ourselves that isn't logical, or rational, but intuitional, with a heavily laden sense and feeling. There are no strict or exact interpretation of our songs, because as one sings, one experiences a full range of emotion and expectation, much of it mysterious, contradictory and paradoxical. There is this need in us for transcendence, for drama, for mystery, and a sort of catharsis through expression. This may be the purest expression of the soul.

The singing and the words associated with the songs become

very pervasive in our thoughts. Even while active in other pursuits, they seem to echo in our inner being, on a seemingly constant basis. This condition seems helpful in making the inner environment ready for growth and change.

Dances in the Indian way involve the total self in prayer and healing. As people dance they sing. In this way the soul receives what it needs most in the form of beauty, mystery, and expression. It is probably the reason for such a sense of fulfillment when one does a good Chinook Dance, or whatever dance done in sincerity and honesty. The body viewed as a fighting machine or a system of reproduction, needs a fuller representation of it purpose. The body has to be honored, play and pleasure is its reward for work. At a much simpler level is simply displaying and expressing God's natural grace in the body. The beauty and mystery in prayer are expressed in rhythm and movement requiring great strength and coordination.

Reconciliation is an everpresent part of healing. One must always be honest, humble, and willing to make things right with ourselves and our fellows. We can sense in ourselves if there is tension or restraint in our relationship with someone else. This tension and restrain prohibits honest and free communication, which is at the heart of a community of sharing. The worst barrier to reconciliation and healthy interaction between individuals is having a judgmental attitude. The start to overcoming this barrier is to have the honesty and humility to recognize that you are judging someone else. Apologies and making amends helps, we are making right our hearts towards another, to the point of asking for forgiveness.

There are some principles we should attend to help overcome perceptions that different procedures mean different fundamental activity. This is important since we are relating spiritual activity of different tribes of Indians.

You pray in your own way, I pray in my own way. We both pray to God. I pray your prayers are answered. Central to all of this is the one God.

We fast and conduct Vision Quests. The important fact

is that we conduct the fast in it fundamental form, the procedures are secondary.

We conduct sweat ceremonies. The important fact is that we sweat and use the sweat to pray, the procedures are secondary.

Procedures and methods are products of personal preference. Personal preference is a product of the ego. There is nothing wrong with the ego, unless it is driven by self centeredness.

Like many spiritual activities paradox is always present. The procedures, which are rituals, are important because they give the beauty and mystery to the procedures. Beauty and mystery are the communication medium of the spirit.

Changing One's Mind

Cosmology refers to a persons overall scheme of reality. Where he or she fits in, where the rest of the people fit it, and the nature of one's relationship to God. Everyone at one or the other develops one. It is the personal philosophy of an individual, or it fits in with his religion, profession, vocation in life, maybe even his politics. The word itself may not be used much by our people, but the concept has always been here.

It is a world view. A problem with our peoples' world view is that it shows that many are prone to depression and hopelessness. This is the overriding nature of powerlessness. The paradoxical nature of powerlessness is that those who don't accept it remain powerless. Those who recognize and accept it, find a source of power outside themselves, and experience a whole new freedom, joy, peace, and empowerment. The other side of the paradox is that when a person surrenders to personal powerlessness, they become empowered from within.

One of the problems in bringing many of the people to heal themselves, is their resistance and mistrust of dogma. There is a natural dislike, among the people we are concerned about, to the idea that there is only one way to do things. Much of this resistance has a lot to do with the ego involvement of the messenger. People will automatically pick up on a prideful or sanctimonious and superior attitude. This is what involving personalities will do to concerted efforts. If we can in humility and without judgement present principles, the message will be more acceptable.

Please do some praying, singing, meditating, and contemplation upon reading the following. Read them with an open mind and an open heart. Try to see the reality and truth in them, because they are intended to be attractive to someone who is down and out.

If you disagree with them simply cross them out and replace

them with a sample of your own. Don't hoard to yourself some of the most important ideas in your life. If we share our most precious gifts, they will be seen and recognized.

If we can avoid the idea that we are going to "save" these unfortunates, there will be communication and exchange. There is no differentiation between them and us. We will learn that at our hearts, we are all one. We are the challenge, we are the problem to be solved. Just like the cartoon charactor Pogo says about meeting and discovering that the enemy is us.

"In the beginning was the Word and the Word was made flesh". Anything people strive or contrive to endeavor starts with ideas and ideals formed in words. It is an action of faith that words come out in an order that will make sense to our fellows. Your ideas and ideals will provide the leverage and fulcrum to move the people. The following are meant to be an example, a framework, or even a guideline.

It is also meant to be a catalyst to stimulate you into developing something similar. Remember, meditation and contemplation are recommended before and after reading the following principles. We have to have serious ideas to attract people to healing. They will have to be able to see if those principles are working in your life. Do you have the peace of mind, the confidence, the hope for the future etc. It will show in your conduct.

Principles of a Good Human Being

Why am I? I am because the Maker decided I should be, and I accept and surrender to that precept. My Maker is Everything, and I am a part of Everything. Where I am-there is my Maker, where there is my Maker-there I am also. **Everything - is in the Earth - in the stars - in my heart.**

Who am I? I am, who I am. I am in the state of becoming more and more of myself. I have been invested with gifts and capabilities that are god-like. I am always growing in the knowledge of how to make good use of these gifts and capabilities. These gifts are: existence, being, awareness, feeling, grace, reverence, remembrance, imagination, motivation, and choice. **I will grow in these gifts thru patience, discipline and effort.**

I am here to live with all the energy and vitality bestowed on me by my Maker.

I don't have a soul, I am the Soul and the soul is not passive. The Soul will speak thru visions and dreams, that are symbolic, that I understand intuitively. It is through Soul that I learn how to use the Maker's Gifts. The soul is the direct connection to the Maker. **My Soul will speak to others thru beauty, in songs, dances, stories, and ceremonies.**

My health and well being are the result of an interaction between the soul, the mind, and the body. **Well-being is an active being, active spiritually, active mentally, active bodily.**

I am responsible for my condition in life, my emotions, my expectations, my dreams and ideals. It is my beliefs about who I am that determine how I will act emotionally, physically, and spiritually. My beliefs about myself, about other persons, about institutions, about reality, about my Maker, shape my values. **My values shape my behavior in my world.**

I am in the world to interact and relate to others like me. The life in this world is a difficult challenge. **The difficulty of the challenges is such so as to be worthy of the abilities I will bring to meet them.**

All of the others persons are individual expressions of their Maker. There are some who will not know this, I will not take advantage them. **I will be a message of hope and possibility to those who don't realize who they are.**

Each person must have an affectionate regard for their unique individuality. **I will not violate the integrity of another, I will not seek to make them feel less than they are.**

I must respect the unique individuality of others. I will be patient and tolerant of other beliefs and systems of spirituality. **If I violate others I will seek reconciliation.**

My individual integrity is inviolable. Just as the Maker gave me many days to experience my life, the Maker gave me many lives to experience myself.

I will conduct myself with honor and dignity that is becoming of a good human being. My code of conduct is based on high personal standards of morality. My conduct will always seriously take into consideration my relationship to my Maker, to others, and to myself.

My potential for goodness is limited only by self-imposed limitations.

My thoughts, emotions, and beliefs are of value to me and my Maker.

I am of supreme value to my Maker, can I value myself any less? Can I value others any less?

I will always pray and meditate to improve my spiritual development. As a good human being, I am a spiritual being.

Pain and dis-ease are teachers, they are powerful allies in the living process of learning how to use the gifts of the Maker.

Again this is a useful meditation to get someone started on the spiritual journey. Contemplation on the meanings of the statements leads a person into some personal insights, and personal revelations. This type of new awareness is happening all the time to people on the path of healing and wholesomeness. It is likely that they won't write them out like I did, mostly it is a personal matter of privacy.

Although some people might use the various prayers and meditations presented here there is no reason for them not to write their own. I have used these as road maps in prayer and meditation. Many people who pray and meditate always find it necessary to quiet the immense activity of the mind. It takes practice to stop consciously thinking, or the incessant chatter of one's inner dialogue.

The interruption of this chatter is necessary to allow us to receive communication from the deepest parts of ourselves and from our Spiritual Guidance. When people say, pray all the time, they mean practice the ability to quiet yourself and receive the communication from your Real Self or God.

Relations

I have come to recognize that I embody much of the damage of a person who has been the object of racism. In a transformation or a spiritual awakening a person acquires the foundation to withstand such serious affronts to human dignity. Our need for healing will be demonstrated in the relationships we have with our fellows. The healing and grieving happen in a community of people with a common experience. A new awareness occurs where we can recognize the God "out there", and also that God actively exists within us. When we can know this, we acquire the dignity and the nobility that is the heritage of the Creator.

As was previously mentioned, we have damage from racism. It is conceivable that the development of social cohesiveness was perverted or mutated. It is likely that we failed to develop those natural skills necessary for close knit families. The symptoms are dysfunctionality of various types such as abuses, violence, compulsive behavior disorders, etc. What we learned with regard to our lack of self esteem and self worth was learned behavior, passed on by previous generations.

I can remember expecting to go through a certain rite of passage when I reached a certain age as I was growing up. As I headed toward maturity I expected that I would kill my first deer and share it with community. I also expected that there would come a time when I would be allowed to get drunk with the elders, until such time I would get drunk with my peers. These were my expectations because this is what I observed when watching the people on which I modelled my behavior.

I was a wife beater. It caused me no small amount of shame and suffering to do such things to someone I supposedly loved. But this is what I learned in the ways to resolve family disputes. If you couldn't work things out, you had to resort to force, (at least this seemed the natural course of events). In relationship of the sexes, the man was expected to dominate. Where did we learn this fundamental idea about one of our more critical relationships?

There are many people among my contemporaries and peers who were victims of abuse, of one sort or another. If a child is treated abusively, that child will learn to be abusive. If a child is treated with love, patience, and understanding, this is what the child learns.

We have many examples of young people committing suicide after the breakup of relationships. Why don't they see the options available to them? Why can't they explore the pain that comes from such occurences, and learn from them? I remember looking at hopelessness of a failed relationship and considering suicide also, I have to admit fear kept me from doing it. Somehow we have to teach our young people that such pain is part of life, part of the risk we take in entering into relationships.

What we seem to be lacking is the inherent respect for each other by the time we reach the age of sexual maturity. I don't recall having anyone teach me about honoring another person who chose to share their life with me. There were never any explanations of loyalty and devotion so necessary to maintain a relationship. Nobody explained to me that there is a tremendous amount of effort required to keep oneself in relationship. We don't learn how to be a friend or a confidant. I wasn't trusted with personal and private information from a so called loved one. I never disclosed any thing that put me at risk. It was after many years of struggle to find some peace in a relationship, that I discovered what intimacy really was.

We have to develope a method to teach our young people that there is such a thing as risk. We have to teach that a lifetime relationship is not a given in our fractured society. We have to teach our young people how th turn to another friend when relationhips fail. I don't think we have learned how to share our pain and disappointment. We should approach the failed relationships much in the same way one grieves for the death in the family. But much of this can be attributed to disfunctionality passed on from previous generations, whose

154

social structure was shattered.

I have witnessed and discussed with my daughter much about relationships. And I think we both have reached the conclusion that relationships don't work if you don't like yourself. We made a joke, "if you're unhappy with yourself, when you get into a relationship, you will make two people unhappy". If we are basically unfulfilled with ourselves, we can't find what is missing in ouselves, in someone else. It places an unfair burden on that person.

Relationships come in may forms. The most painful are the sexual relationships that produce children. We have many children that weren't a consideration prior to their conception. Much of the abuse comes because a young mother sees the child as a restraint to her having fun. A child mustn't be held accountable for the irresponsibility of immature parents, who may be still children themselves. But we see evidence that children pay the consequences.

Key to children's development is the development and the encouragement of invdividuality. A person can't go through the mating rituals under the paradigm of looking for a lost father or a lost mother. One can't go through the process looking for a care giver. We have to have healthy parents to produce healthy children. Much of this can occur if our young people would go through a passage where they would ask a key question of themselves. And if they entered this process, they didn't conclude it until they were comfortable with themselves, and able to be with themselves as a friend to themselves. This key question is, "who am I?" Relatedness means we understand that we stand separate from others as equals. In this we must understand that we have similarities that allow us to help each other, that we have differences that allow us to compliment each other.

In discussing the relationship with ourselves it is hard to separate the relationship to the Creator. Maybe there isn't a separation. We have been greatly blessed by being created into a beautiful and awesome world. Our physical reality has so much wonder, and so much to learn about its nature, we forget where it is at it's source. We can get caught up in worry, fear, and guilt, or the competition. In this way we forget our true selves which is spiritual and closely aligned with God. Our relationship with God should become one where we quiet the distractions and our own minds, and relax to connect with our Source.

To be in a relationship we have to recognize that we are individuals with a unique and distinctive identity relative to something or someone else. Relationships probably don't happen if we can't see that we are separate and unique from others.

Our problems with ourselves probably started with what we mistakenly thought was our relationship to others. It is no surprise that recovery is directly proportional to amount and degree of our tolerance and acceptance others. As we acquire dignity there appears in our makeup forgiveness and empathy. As we acquire dignity we learn true pride which is a high regard for our own individuality. As we acquire dignity we recognize that the God that fires our existence, burns in the hearts of our fellows, this is true humility. When a person says they have a problem with anger, they really have a problem with a lack of dignity, - a lack of patience and tolerance. A person who acquires dignity, is possessed with the noble bearing of someone with immense patience and tolerance. This person will not only accept and tolerate differences among individuals, but will celebrate the variety that is life.

One of the more beautiful ceremonies conducted in the Cursillo was a blessing. The candidates were taught to extend their hands towards the object of their blessing and sing in unison:

"May the Spirit of the Lord be upon you,

We bless you in the name of the Lord"

This was sung to the tune of "I Wish I Was and Oscar Meyer Wiener". This is a sublime act of generosity, because how could you want anything more for someone. This is a very important practice since the person sending, is sending from deep within the self. This was repeated each time a person was before them to give a talk or share.

In the Bible there are the Ten Commandments. One is to honor ones parents, or "Honor your father and your mother".

This is the way we affirm our connectedness with everything else.   Through our parents we are connected to our ancestors, who are connected to the "Circle of Life", which is the evolutionary chain of the spirit, which binds us with the evolutionary chain of life, connected to evolutionary chain of matter, back to the Source. Chief Seattle has referred to this as the "Web of life, whatever we do unto the web of life, we do to ourselves." We honor the earth who combines with the Sun to sustain us.

Nothing will drive a person crazier than one's own offspring. You think, "You can't be my child, you're totally different!" Which is the literal truth. Much of the problem stems from our perception that our children are an extension of ourselves. They truly are "Totally different!" They are individuals in their own right, not because we grant it, simply because they are.   They remind us that God has allowed us to share in that wonderful creational activity, making life. As a life unto themselves they got to be "Totally different." It is through them we are given the opportunity to extend the best that we can find in ourselves, if we have the patience, tolerance, and acceptance, or if we have the dignity.

The infatuations that many of our young people and even some of the so called mature people, get involved in, is the confusion of infatuation with love. The culture of the T.V. and music oriented society emphasize finding our one "True Love". We think we have found it when we experience the tremendous stimulation and excitement from another person.   Many of our young people enter into a supposedly life time commitment based on these ideas and sentiments. The relationships based on feelings of infatuation change or end, and some of our young ones feel that their life is over. They need to understand that endings are an important part of the life experience. Love is too important to life to be limited to sexual relationships.   The feelings that come with the termination of infatuational relationships are painful, but feelings are just the flavor or color of our reality. At these times we need to separate our feelings about reality and reality itself. Youngsters should be warned that there are going to be these periods when they enter into "Puppy

Love". They should also be warned about "falling in love".

We feel our emotions arise, because they are expected to arise within ourselves, based on our beliefs that they should. We can change these expectations and beliefs, about what feelings we need to experience and express. Looked at this way we can avoid the fatalism of thinking we are the victims of falling, when in fact we are jumping into love. We have a decision or choice in the matter. We can explain to our young ones and some of our immature older ones, whose world has ended, that a person can jump out of this condition by consciously deciding to do so.

The spouse, if we're someone's spouse we have decided that we will enter into long term commitment. It has to be long term because the purpose of this type of relationship is to have children, and to become a family. Infatuation is a starting point of these unions, but such unions are not static. In spite of both spouses best efforts, the union is one of dynamic change. Enter into one with dignity, for at the heart of this union is the love of true friendship. The changes that come with the relationship need to be taught to those entering into them. Many think that when the infatuation is over the union is over. It is only entering to a fuller more healthier phase. The "I" in these unions has to subjugate itself to the "We", to the point that the individual identity starts with the we.

Leadership is probably the most difficult and rewarding activity a person can undertake. Preparation is through a quest for dignity, becoming the good human being, practicing the way of the warrior, and acquiring wisdom. The central activity here is making choices, or decisions. All the choices or decisions a leader makes is to fulfill the mission and purpose of those being lead. A leader must possess honesty and integrity, for those being lead to accept direction. A leader must have developed the "Wisdom" and the way of the "Warrior" and be motivated by the "Higher Purpose", to be an example and set the pattern of behavior for those lead. And in one those paradoxes in life, if the leader acts selfless in leadership, the self grows and flourishes, and the leader becomes even more of a leader. The leader not only exemplifies but articulates the hopes, vision, and aspirations of those lead. And in another paradox dominates those lead with greater hopes, and farther vision, and more profound aspirations, through a highly centered ego.

Riders on the Storm

There are legends and myths from some of the Plains Indian Tribes that tell of a mythical warrior who rode the tornadoes and cyclones. It is unfortunate that much of these stories are lost to our young people. For the tornadoes and cyclones are metaphors for life in general, and we can greatly use them to prepare young people for life.

The tornadoes and cyclones, in the stories represent the awesome natural forces in life. The circumstances and challenges in life are unpredictable and often overwhelming. It seems their only purpose is causing you turmoil, and uprooting you from tranquility. The tornadoes and cyclones are terrifying and awesome. They represented the extreme in natural forces uncontrolled and unleashed. And yet the warrior rode them because he had the ability to ride them. The warrior accepted the challenge of riding storms and proving himself a worthy opponent.

We are the riders on the storm of life. We are blessed with the ability to meet any challenge. Our Maker did not cast us here naked and helpless, without resources to meet and ride the storm. It isn't blind chance that we encounter the storms, we are meant to meet them, and we are meant to ride them. Our Maker wants us to experience the thrill and excitement of riding. We are meant to test and learn about everything we possess in terms of human capacity to meet and overcome difficult rides. By doing this we affirm that the Maker's creations are good. We should rejoice when we are confronted with a challenge. In the back of our minds we should hear "this one's for you!" We should become excited at the prospect of discovering something new about ourselves. Some new ability we never would have uncovered, or discovered, had we not been challenged.

There have been accounts of our ancestral warriors and leaders praying to their Maker, giving thanks and expressing gratitude for being blessed with strong enemies. The strong enemy forced you to become just as strong, just as courageous, with just as much intestinal fortitude. The prospect of strong enemies disciplined the warrior to make himself vigorous and full of vitality, to be always preparing for the next opponent. The warrior was proud to prove himself worthy of living. While proving personal worthiness the warrior experienced the joy of living.

There were the times when the warrior did not overcome the challenges. This was viewed as an opportunity to learn, to identify weaknesses in attitude or practice, as an opportunity to adjust and make adaptations. It was in this way the warrior was always reminded that the most serious challenges in living, were within the warrior's own self.

The challenges that exist within the person might fall under the broad category of self-pity. Or they might be self-deception. When a person thinks they lack the courage, they generally mean they deny their own inherent ability, or refuse to see or accept some personal responsibility. Perhaps they are too filled with false pride to ask their Maker for guidance and help, which will be always given. The lack of courage is the lack of the will to act. In many cases this is just a refusal to make a choice or a decision.

Affirmation is the positive response to challenge, mindful of being the "worthy opponent". It is possessing the courage and willingness to bring the best of our abilities and effort to meet challenge. When viewed this way, there appears no difference between life and challenge. We thank the Creator for our life, we thank the Creator for our challenges because they shape us and make us grow.

When a person asks one's self the important questions in life, there is always the question, "why is there evil". In examining our past one hundred and fifty years, I've asked myself, "Why did the Creator allow this to happen?". People will always confront such questions with answers that are vague and unsatisfactory to our logical rational mind. We are confronting a mystery, we are involving ourselves in life, we are facing the challenge. The mystery is a sign that we are on the right path, and we have come to a critical juncture. There is no incorrect answer to such profound questions, the key is putting onself in position to confront them.

In the quest to become a good human being, the journey is as important as the destination. Along the way we can bring forth what our ancestors brought forth naturally, that spiritual being within, that is our true self. Those abilities suppressed by an oppressive culture will be regained. Ask the questions like the one just asked, that answers will come if we pay attention to our true self. Life has great meaning and will disclose a purpose for what our people have gone through. There are highly useful abilities and skills developed by our people as the result of our experience. It is possible that we have an opportunity to take the worst we have experienced and make it an asset we can use to help other people.

Grandfather! I come here today -

To pray to the Creator and the Great Grandmother-

In that place You gave to our people -

To come and talk to You -

To ask for the things we need -

In the Great Grand Mother's womb -

Where we are reunited with Her -

Where we are cleansed and purified -

Where we are reborn -

We pray to give thanks for the gift of life -

The gift of life we receive today, - now -

What we do with that life is our gift to You in return -

I pray I'm worthy of my gift -

I pray I'm worthy of living.

Grandfather, these are your words,

Expressed through me and my life.

About the Author

Mr. Joseph is a 48 year-old Native American, a Coville Confederated Tribes member, who has lived on the reservation since birth. He was educated at the University of Washington and received his degree in business administration. He has experienced the recovery written about.